MODERN-DAY LIBERALISM:

EXPLORING THE PSYCHOLOGICAL FOUNDATIONS OF THE DISORDER

J. D. MITSCHKE

MODERN-DAY LIBERALISM:
Exploring the Psychological Foundations of the Disorder

World Ahead Press is a division of WND Books. The views and opinions expressed in this book are those of the author and do not necessarily reflect the official policy or position or WND Books.

Paperback ISBN: 978-1-944212-12-4
eBook ISBN: 978-1-944212-13-1

Printed in the United States of America
16 17 18 19 20 21 XXX 9 8 7 6 5 4 3 2 1

ACKNOWLEDGEMENTS

I am grateful to those whose work and influence was instrumental in assisting me in the formation of many of the ideas and concepts presented in this book. Some were close friends and associates while others, though not known to me personally, yet served as invaluable sources of teaching and knowledge. The common denominator which we all shared was the insatiable desire to arrive at objective knowledge and a valid science as it pertained to the psychology of individual human life on this earth. Indeed there are lawfully designed and perennially manifesting characteristics indelibly woven into the warp and woof of this fabric of dynamic potential of each and every individual. Special thanks to: Martha J. Barham, PhD, Jay W. Barham, Maurice Nicoll, P. D. Ouspensky, G. I. Gurdjieff, Rodney Collin, C. G. Jung, Milton H. Erickson, Aenka, and Mario.

CONTENTS

INTRODUCTION

There isn't a definition of mental illness in existence that would lend itself in a few brief words to a universal understanding of the term. Anyone who has sought for an answer to this query, what is a mental illness, may have found a number of subjective classifications and descriptions of mental disorders, but generally such definitions only serve to open doors to further beg the question. One may as well try to define *mental illness* by saying, it is a *psychological disorder*—this tells us nothing to further our understanding. A clearly definable common ground upon which a definition may rest is not to be found that would concisely set forth in a brief sentence or two the foundation for a satisfactory understanding. It does not exist.

Accepting this to be the truth of the matter, the entire milieu of mental health and mental illness—the science of which rests upon at best a great deal of subjectivity—presents special challenges to both the lay person and the professional as they all attempt to understand it, treat those who are mentally ill, and converse or write about the issue.

Clearly, the fact that we do not yet fully understand it does not get in the way of an entire service industry of professionals forming around it to treat those who are mentally ill.

Collectively, we as a culture and those in the profession of mental health continue to make various conclusions about mental illnesses regarding the etiology of how a mental illness manifests; and then, how do we set about to define the extreme of mental illness or the notion of insanity? One has only to think of the many court cases in which the defense team laboriously evaluates whether there is enough pathology to put forth the insanity plea for their client, sometimes successful and sometimes not amidst all the hair-splitting.

But the diagnosis, treatments, and interventions of the mentally ill continue uninterrupted as if we already have within our grasp a thorough understanding of it. If it were a fact that the science of mental health was clearly identified and established, then why has it happened that over the past number of decades, new pop therapies and various treatment modalities crop up—become the current craze in the treatment industry—and just as quickly vanish and fall out of favor?

For example, I once heard from a reliable source that the notions put forth in the book, *I'm OK, You're OK*—very popular in the late 1960s and well into the 1970s, with over 15,000,000 copies in print, and boasting to have helped millions of people—this book was created upon the basis of a gentleman's bet—that is, one person said to another, "I'll bet you cannot come up with a new therapy." Well, the person did come up with a new therapy. But where is it now? Are therapists and counselors today across our country using the methods set forth in the book? No, of course not. Let me know if you find someone who is. Many new or used copies of the book are still plentiful on Amazon.com, or perhaps you may run across one for even less money, gathering dust at your local thrift store.

If the above conclusions are correct— the implications of this are far-reaching. If our understanding of mental illness is so lacking; then our understanding of the working components of this marvelous God-created piece of machinery, otherwise called the human being—from the study of which we attempt to base an understanding of mental illness— may be just as lacking.

It is from this conclusion that the content of this book will develop a framework. The aim of this book is to explore the foundations and manifestations of modern-day liberalism; explore the working dynamics of the human being from a psychological, developmental, and environmental perspective, and once and for all time uncover the truth behind the statement already spoken and written that *liberalism is a mental disorder*, or the variant, *liberalism is a psychological disorder*. If coming up with a definition of mental illness evades us, then, it is just as likely that to freely associate liberalism with a mental disorder and formulate a definition of liberalism the mental disorder—poses a like challenge to us. But despite that—we'll gladly take on that challenge.

For well over four decades, I immersed myself in the study and practice of various therapeutic modalities in the milieu of mental health. I was driven by an insatiable appetite to explore and fully understand especially the psychological, behavioral, mental, physical, and spiritual aspects of this marvelous though complicated piece of machinery called the human being.

Because this introduction begins with a focus on mental illness, it is only natural to direct our attention to the comprehensive reference manual generally subscribed to by those who are in the practice of psychological counseling and therapeutic interventions. This reference manual I am referring to is the *Diagnostic and Statistical Manual of Mental Disorders*, otherwise referred to simply as the DSM. Though created as a guidebook to help professionals in the understanding and treatment of mental illnesses; many professionals in that setting will tell you that the DSM still remains an imperfect guidebook. It does not definitively tell us what a mental illness is. And what may be of further surprise to all, it has nothing to do with statistics; as if a definition of mental illness could be extrapolated from statistics.

The DSM, now in its seventh decade of existence (the DSM-I was first published in 1952), has gone through a number of revisions. Each major revision was identified by the use of a Roman numeral, starting with the DSM-I, then II, then III, and so on. For the most part, I was more closely associated and familiar with the DSM-IV, which was published in 1994 and remained in use until the next major revision and publication in 2013 of the DSM-5. The new revision of the DSM-5 represents a complete dramatic shift, upheaval, reordering, and with many deletions of all the various disorders formerly found in the previous DSMs. The new DSM will be oriented primarily to neuroscience and biological reductionism; that is, no longer will your mental illness be grounded primarily in factors that are environmental, developmental, or emotional, but rather for the reason that one has something wrong with their physical brain. Therefore, all that may be needed for one to do is pop a pill to fix it. You may notice that the latest revision dropped the identifier of the Roman numeral and used instead the Arabic numerical system, hence, 5 instead of V. There's a reason for the change to the Arabic system. Because further minor revisions are anticipated to come about regularly with the DSM, that is, 5 becomes 5.1, 5.2, and so forth; computer programs just do not understand nor know how to read or deal with the antiquated Roman numeral revision system of 'V' to 'V.I', for example... revisionism... so much for things steadfast and enduring in mental health. Also, in keeping with the 'new world ordering', the new DSM represents a streamlining, synthesis, and coordination of mental health with the new delivery of medical healthcare; then, synchronizing with the International Classification of Diseases (ICD-10). And lastly, all of this is aimed at smoother consolidation and synchronization under the huge enveloping umbrella of the World Health Organization. And guess what else is a key ingredient to this configuration? That's right *The Affordable Care Act*, otherwise known as Obamacare, which we know Obama neither wrote nor read. Yes indeed, mental health still remains a science, and to borrow a term from Maslow, is still seeking *self-actualization*, if it is even possible for an inanimate thing to do that.

The focus of this book is not to explore the history of the DSM and mental health; neither is it designed to exhaustively explore the development and history of liberalism as it unfolded starting over three hundred years ago, but rather to focus on modern-day liberalism as we find it in our current era.

Fundamental differences exist when comparing the foundation of the word *liberal*, what it originally meant, with the meaning of liberal as we find it today. The root of the word liberal comes from the word *liberty*. Most everyone espouses liberty, right? Liberal originally meant that every man and woman should be free to pursue their interests supported on the foundation of liberty, equality, and justice. This is all fine and well, but somewhere along the way, liberal entered the realm of the political and then the bastardization of the standards for which the word stood for began to be distorted. Politicians and the government then usurped the role of dispensing liberty and doing what they considered best for the masses and the electorate, and based upon what they proclaimed were the presumed needs of the status quo, or upon their perceived notion of what the problems were that needed to be addressed. But to pull off this heist, the politicians also needed a willing and malleable, if not a downright passive, acquiescing electorate.

As the notions of the term liberal evolved, it was during this evolvement and transformation that the suffix *ism* became attached to the word liberal, now making it *liberalism*. Anytime the suffix ism is added to a word, be wary. You will know by this act that a doctrine, creed, or something dogmatic has just been ushered in.

For example, take the word *commune*. We all know what a commune is. Simply defined, it's a gathering of people, usually a smaller collection of people, sharing things in common; whether property, possessions, income, assets, sharing common care and looking out for one another, et cetera. It's sort of like the traditional nuclear American family with the one difference being that the parents are in charge. I grew up in a large family; I suppose we were sort of like a commune. Many of you Americans having grown up in a traditional American nuclear family may have experienced some of these basic communal characteristics. Then, in the sixties, it became fashionable that communes sprang up to include groups larger than and include those outside of blood family ties. Okay, fine and well; to each their own. Maybe it works for them and as long as all participants were of one accord. But when the practice begins to grow and evolve, when its application becomes doctrinaire and mandatory, and the practice of instituting communal existence has been subject to the usurpation of authoritarian government and those holding power and authority, we have *communism*. And we can all see how well that has worked out in communist Russia, China, North Korea, or Cuba. As a general rule, anytime the suffix ism or *ian* becomes attached to a word, a devolvement has occurred leading to meanings that are now doctrinaire and authoritarian—displacing the original meaning of the term. It is partly on this basis that we will advance our discussion of the foundation of modern-day liberalism.

Across this great land of America reside countless citizens, many desiring to remain informed about news, events, and people in the domain of the national political and governing arena. The degree of participation by the populace varies. Some are satisfied to stay informed only in a superficial manner. Others monitor closely the words and actions of our elected officials holding political office—observing the greater- and lesser-known news pundits, commentators, and journalists in all the various media outlets, as they put forth a steady continuous stream of continuously changing newsworthy headlines—all in an effort to be among the fully informed.

Many of this audience of citizens are likely well aware that battling it out in this arena of national issues, ideals, ideas, words, and actions, are two main opposing camps. They are known by the names, *conservatives* and *liberals*. Generally, Republicans are associated with the conservative camp and Democrats with the liberal camp.

This ongoing battle, often identified as an ideological battle, regularly heats up to a fever pitch, and concomitant with that battle is interjected all the legislative and political bias, the political ploys, the innuendos, accusations, threats, epithets and name-calling, and out-and-out lies—endlessly hurled at one side and then the other—all in all, creating quite a spectacle.

Likely you've heard of different pejorative labels applied to both these separate camps. Conservatives are sometimes referred to as *right-wing, far right wingers,* or *guns and Bible clingers,* and the well-known conservative movement known as the "Tea Party" are called *tea-baggers.* The liberals, on the other hand, are known by such terms as *left-wing, secular progressives, leftists,* or *deranged leftists,* and are accused of having a mental disorder or a psychological disorder. And that's just a sampling of the various terms.

And to all those many American citizens across our nation, who, if questioned sincerely, a good number I'm sure, may also reveal that they closely identify ideologically with the one camp or the other, which is, either as a *liberal* or a *conservative.* At one time in your life you may have been asked by someone, "Are you a liberal or a conservative?" If so, what was your answer? Do you see yourself as more closely aligned with one or the other?

Regarding how the actual numbers of conservatives and liberals sort out, I reject the notion that the numbers are evenly (or even closely) divided. There is a huge contingent of the silent majority which is seldom heard from and it is argued that if pressed with enough direct questions on the many polarizing issues, they would reveal themselves as leaning conservative. The problem is—there is too much passivity and not enough engagement of passion and positive aggression on their part.

It's an accurate generalization that conservatives tend to be more accepting and non-confrontational to opposing points of view. If they were to fully engage their passion (passion is another name for emotion under which the emotion of anger may be included), it could possibly result in a tidal wave of resistance against the liberal-progressive agenda that is decimating our nation. Perhaps one day those passive conservatives will engage themselves to take action and befriend some righteous *anger* to serve them as a personal ally to resist the onslaught of liberalism. Observe how even though we are well over a year away from the national general election, the numbers of people lining up with Donald Trump far exceed those of his opponents for the reason that Trump is passionately espousing issues of which resonate with conservative leanings; leaving aside for the moment any arguments of whether or not Trump is a true conservative.

Many arguments have already been put forth by writers, commentators, and news pundits pointing out the bias of the mainstream media that favors modern liberalism and progressive points of view over those leaning towards conservatism. Hence, the mainstream media would like us all to believe that liberalism dominates in numbers of support and influence. It is because many liberals scream and rant and rave the loudest, and their disproportionate emotionality often operates at a fever pitch. One only needs to recall a shrill screaming episode of Hillary Rodham Clinton, the famous scream of Howard Dean, or the screams and screeches of an entourage of Code Pink, just to give a few examples. A perception is created in the minds of many that their numbers are far greater than they actually are and surely they must outnumber the conservatives. But it is a fallacious notion that liberals dominate in number. Well over fifty years ago the Swiss psychologist C. G. Jung pointed to the fallacy of this misguided perception (of liberal domination) when he wrote,

> *The relatively small percentage of the population figures they represent is more than compensated for by the peculiar dangerousness of these people. Their mental state is that of a collectively excited group ruled by affective judgments and wish-fantasies. In a milieu of this kind they are the adapted ones, and consequently they feel quit at home in it. They know from their own experience the language of these conditions, and they know how to handle them. Their chimerical ideas, sustained by fanatical resentment, appeal to the collective irrationality and find fruitful soil there; they express all those motives and resentments which lurk in more normal people under the cloak of reason and insight. They are therefore, despite their small number in comparison with the population as a whole, dangerous as sources of infection precisely because the so-called normal person possesses only a limited degree of self knowledge.* "[1]

I don't believe it's a fact at all that the liberals dominate in number. In reality, the mainstream media is more likely to cover the gatherings and rallies of liberals as they spew forth their liberal propaganda and often exaggerates and slants the circumstances and inflates the numbers that turn out. On the contrary, the mainstream media seldom turn out in as great a number as at a conservative event, and if they do, they generally focus on any small facet of the event to mischaracterize it!

Nevertheless, despite the liberals actually being outnumbered, which I believe is the case, the damage they do is in direct proportion to the high volume and emotionality of their ranting and raving and the disruptions that result. The intense magnitude of the emotional hatred and anger they generate as it reverberates among the masses, and all the ubiquitous lies they spread—many of which are woven into the many tenets and laws of governance, their relentless push to political correctness, and the reporting bias of the mainstream media—added together create a powerful suggestive factor to the general public, that the strength of their liberal message and their numbers are far greater than they actually are.

Assuming their actual numbers to be exaggerated and inflated, the liberal's many shallow and baseless rants and slogans, however, continue unabated as sources of infectious ideas which unfortunately find fertile ground among the vulnerable and suggestible among the masses—thereby increasing the numbers who succumb to their point of view, and consequently readily chime in as participants in the highly emotionalized ranting and raving. And why do so many succumb to this? It's because reason and logic (preempted by heightened and distorted emotionality) is unfortunately not necessarily fully engaged in many of whom are presumed to be, 'normal persons' of the electorate. Then, all in all, the perception is created that the actual numbers of the liberal's and their relative strength are far greater than they really are.

Indeed, it is an ideological battle creating the great divide that is fracturing our nation. It is a puzzlement how we as a population—all the millions of individuals composing our nation—can be separated by such a wide gulf of disparity. How does it happen in regard to a specific issue—so many issues really, that there can exist such a positioning of polar opposites on any specific issue?

Those in leadership are certainly not exempt from this split and fracturing in our culture, for it is either by will-full choice or by unconscious mechanically driven behavior that they are part of the fray. It may be argued that they play the key role as the instigators and catalysts of it. And the unfortunate fallout is that our Constitution, and our founding principles and ideals are adversely compromised. How is it that whether it is among the least, or the most hotly contested issues, there cannot be an acknowledgement that by the infusion of reason, logic, common sense, and facts, the contested issue may be resolved with a clear-cut answer or a solution? What is it that's driving these irrational beliefs of the liberal?

Well, perhaps we can sort out an answer to this question in the coming pages, and then many of the multitudes of people, who for the most part remain silent and passive, and witness the carnage taking place from a distance, will learn they may cease making that wailing mournful cry, said with an attitude of slavish defeatism, "Why can't we all just get along?" Visualize these words spoken with 'Kumbaya' softly playing in the background. In my view, these are the voices of the meek and the moderates. They are moderate because they just want to get along. "Let's just compromise and get along," they say. Yeah, right—as if some moderate is going to come riding in on a white horse and save the day! Moderates generally prefer to ride fences—not white horses and in the final analysis—don't stand steadfastly and completely for one thing or another. One may as well play the part of a referee to a room-full of individuals composed of both moderate drunkards and moderate Alcoholics Anonymous members, who are contesting each other over what should be considered moderation in their consumption of alcohol. Will a constructive resolution ever come of it?—likely not. In either case, the AA member violates their principle and the drunkard violates their lack of principle. Both compromise themselves, rendering each one ineffective to achieve their objective.

Why do you think that both liberal and conservative politicians—come election time—water down and modify their respective positions and points of view? Well … they want the vote of the wishy-washy moderate as well as the support of their respective right or left contingency. This ploy by the political candidate also reveals their chameleonic nature towards disingenuousness and dishonesty, and really, a lack of steadfast principle.

Some issues deserve a steadfast position either one way or another. I know it's getting worn out, but like the old saying goes, "If you stand for nothing—you will fall for anything." The Constitution cannot be halfway decimated with the expectation that our nation will survive. Our Bill of Rights cannot be decimated without the entire structural edifice being weakened. It sometimes appears that many of the American citizenry are but passive powerless viewers on the sidelines watching events and life unfold before them, and come 'at' them, having accepted and surrendered to the belief they are powerless to do anything about it… no ability, or worse, no desire to participate fully to do anything about circumstances or events.

My intent in presenting this book is to show that this fracturing divide or the line of demarcation between the conservatives and liberals is not as clear cut and definable as one may imagine or assume. We will learn that the symptoms of liberal tendencies cross far over into both sides of that imaginary and unidentifiable line of demarcation that presumably separates the liberals and conservatives. Defining a liberal or a conservative presents as much challenge as defining mental illness.

In the coming discussion, no one will be spared scrutiny, but it may happen that those individuals occupying upper levels of leadership and the media pundits will get the greater spotlight of attention and not necessarily in a flattering manner—because of the fact that they carry much more notoriety due to their visibility in the public eye and because they claim to be leaders or voices of the people … they will be taken to task.

All the elected leadership throughout our country—from the president, Congress, and senators on the national level down the hierarchy of governance at the state level, and even farther down the scale of governing bodies (yes, from the president on down) **all** are elected servants of we the people and thereby should practice exemplary behavior and adhere in the utmost to principles of truth, virtue, and honesty, and diligently work to uphold the oath they took upon being elected, and swore to uphold, that is, "To guard and protect the Constitution of the United States of America."

Have you, dear reader, stopped to deeply reflect and analyze these various dynamics and any relevance they might have in regard to your own point of view and beliefs?

And for purposes of full disclosure, here at the very beginning, I hereby reveal the fact that should I be called upon to self-identify as belonging to one camp or the other, then yes, I consider myself a conservative.

My hope is that once you've completed the reading of this book and fully understand the material, if I have done my job properly, you will come to the full realization that of the three—conservative, liberal, or moderate—by definition, only a conservative could objectively address these issues, given the fact that liberals and moderates are lacking when it comes to producing objectivity and reason. So, therefore, how can the two latter be a reliable source of information?

But you, dear reader, can determine that on your own. Therefore I urge you not to pre-judge me and this material here at the beginning, but rather take the information as given; read it thoroughly and reflect upon it. The material will call upon you to do some reflection both inward to yourself, and outward in observance of people and the world at large. My hope is that it will supply you with new knowledge and new information, and will assist you to build a new perspective of both yourself and others—and the world and nation in which you live, and of how you may be infused with new motivation to interact with the world around you in a positive, proactive manner.

CHAPTER 1

LIBERALS AND CONSERVATIVES— LAYING THE GROUNDWORK

Both of these variations, *liberalism is a mental disorder*, or, *liberalism is a psychological disorder,* point to the same basic condition.

It is my steadfast conviction that modern-day liberalism is grounded in a psychological disorder—the consequences of which result in maladaptive behavior characterized by individuals making choices that result in poor outcomes disadvantageous to all concerned— and the foundation from which those choices proceed are grounded in skewed reasoning and faulty logic. Despite all the various attempts—much talked about and discussed—to specifically define and fully explain exactly how this phenomenon, condition, abnormality, sickness, call it what you will, establishes itself in the psyche of the individual—still deserves much more scrutiny and analysis.

While the colloquial nomenclature submits this very brief definition of liberalism, that is, *liberalism is a mental disorder*—the submission of just a few words cannot suffice as a comprehensive definition that will enable one to gain a thorough understanding of it. This definition lacks basic substance and takes the notion no farther too exhaustively explain the dynamics at play.

So then, unfortunately, the only thing available for the consumption by the attentive masses is nothing more than an incomplete understanding of the disorder—and to very many, there will continue a yearning for the truth and understanding of what drives this condition.

Conservatives and Republicans will continue to accuse the liberals of having this disorder when all the while they do not fully understand what it is themselves, although they may claim to identify it when they think they see it; make judgments about it based upon results and outcomes; and are seemingly content to have a descriptive word or two serve as a substitute (and a very poor substitute at that) for a thorough understanding of it. Their definitions generally tend to terminate upon the simple labeling of specific behaviors.

Often, those who discuss and write about liberalism focus more on the symptoms than on the causative factors that actually create the condition of liberalism. In other words, dialog and actions, the direction of activity, specific activities and events, and end results alone tend to define what liberalism is. It's sort of like discussing and defining the foundation of influenza by describing myriad symptoms the person may have—fever, headache, nausea, lack of appetite, et cetera—and that, it is concluded, defines what the flu is. But then omitting to note that the cause of these symptoms is an intrusive virus, having originated from a specific place, which somehow entered the body and began to infect this or that.

It's unfortunate that liberalism is not caused by a virus. Then we could simply identify it, isolate it, and treat it! But it's not that simple.

Just as many conservatives dislike being called extreme right wingers, neither do many liberals like to be called a liberal. Many chronically afflicted liberals remain in complete denial when accused of having this condition and vehemently rebel against such an accusation. Is it because they don't like labels or just want to hide from what they are?

Even if the chronically afflicted liberals suspected they had this disorder, if only in accordance with their limited understanding based on the incomplete way it's currently defined and portrayed, many don't have the desire or ability, nor does it occur to them to identify their predispositions to liberalism and then rid themselves of it.

Then, there are those liberals who when accused of being a liberal gladly accept the label and wear it proudly as a badge of honor. They have no desire to be other than a liberal, and therefore see no need to engage in any introspection and self-examination. Evidently, they have achieved a certain comfort zone—find comfort and security in identifying with those of like characteristics as themselves or perhaps even consider themselves as among the elite—and have no need to move from that position.

Questions may arise as we all try to come to an understanding of what's involved in this mental disorder.

It seems that any time a reference is made to mental disorder or mental illness, attention is immediately shifted to the brain, as indeed the brain is the domain of one's thinking and it is automatically assumed the brain is the source of the problem. In fact, in accordance with the revised framework of the DSM–5, this is the very notion that we are supposed to accept.

Is the condition of liberalism limited strictly to the mental component of the total person, as there seems to be an automatic assumption that the disorder stems from the mental? Does it mean something is awry in the brain, suggesting an organic or hereditary cause? What about the other major components of a person's complete existential structure in what I recognize in an individual as a Four Component System, composed of; the physical, the emotional, the intellectual (mental), and the spiritual? Do any of these other components play a role as part of the foundation of this condition of liberalism?

Of course, while our primary focus is on the mental, may we take it as a given that reference to the mental and the intellect are describing the very same organ, the function of which is organically based in the physical gray matter of the brain? May we leave aside all organically or genetically based problems in the brain as possible causes of this disorder and presume that this disorder is rooted exclusively in individualized factors that are developmental, environmental, and psychological? If so, good!

The next step then is to determine in what manner these factors constellate into certain brands of behavior in the overall experience of the individual, ultimately leading to what we identify as the disorder of liberalism. It is imperative also to determine what role, if any, the other three components (that is, the physical, emotional, and the spiritual) play in the formation of the disorder. If we do that, then we may move forward in an effort to come to an understanding of this disorder. Then there is a chance we may get to the root cause driving the arguments and conflicts which form the basis of so many of the contentious issues which have reached a fever pitch between the liberals and conservatives.

It is very important to establish that this malady of liberalism not only afflicts those who identify with the Democratic Party, which is the overriding misaligned assumption. Much to the chagrin of some, which may especially surprise and shock the Republicans, the sickness of liberalism is non-partisan. Just because a person self-identifies as Republican, does not mean that person is a fully functioning conservative. For many decades, Republicans have come to be associated with conservative. That is no longer accurate, as many have gradually strayed from their roots. Now we have RINOs (Republican in Name Only) and the various strains of neo-conservatives. But the transformation and evolution has reached a critical stage. I will overlay an identifier and in referring to both of these just mentioned; the new name is CINO, Conservative in Name Only. I hereby coin this new term, CINO. Frankly, I don't think we can accurately even use the acronym RINO any longer because the Republican Party has morphed into something almost unrecognizable from what it once was!

When one really thinks about it, they're a bunch of closet liberals, and speedily, one by one, they are all coming out of the closet! Perhaps a name change for the Republican Party would be in order or maybe a spirit of transformation may miraculously infuse itself into the Republican Party.

Liberalism may just as easily afflict those who identify with the Republican Party, Independents, or those who align with any other party or ideology; or it may afflict those who have no political or ideological affiliation whatsoever. So, for that matter, anyone may be subject to this affliction to a varying degree!

Just because someone self-identifies as being a liberal or a conservative, do not for a moment believe that the individual is a purist as belonging completely to one camp or the opposite one. No. Not at all! But in fairness, even a liberal may on occasion identify with a conservative viewpoint.

Consider the likes of Mitch McConnell, John Boehner, or Jeb Bush. They claim to be conservative, but from observing their behavior, it often appears they have little idea what it means. Jeb Bush as of now is being groomed as a potential frontrunner of the Republican Party for the presidential election of 2016. But he is totally lost when it comes to immigration. He believes, "Great countries need to secure their border for national security purposes, for economic purposes and for rule of law purposes."[1]

That position is fine and well. But then, recently he stated (and I'm paraphrasing), that borders are not so much about keeping people out—but rather keeping people with bad intent in. Really, Jeb, how can two such notions—one completely incongruous to reality—occupy the same brain? That's characterizing the United States of having a prison-like condition. Then why are so many trying to get in to the United States of America? Stalinist Russia created a wall to keep both good and bad people in, and I don't believe there were great numbers clamoring about at the walls to get in, but many did indeed want out.

Jeb Bush, like so many other RINOs and CINOs, takes his cue depending upon who or what group he is addressing, like so many politicians who raise their finger in the air to test the direction of the political winds to which they can then re-adapt their thinking, feeling, and behavior. Recently at a Telemundo interview, Jeb Bush speaking entirely in Spanish told the anchor Jose Diaz-Balart that he was hurt by GOP presidential primary rival Donald Trump's comments about illegal immigrants from Mexico.[2] Even Jeb Bush's posture and demeanor took on the characteristics of one who is hurt; that is, a sad look that is crying out, "Give me pity."

Dear reader, there is no such naturally occurring human emotion as that of "feeling hurt". This strategy of feigning "feeling hurt" is a manipulation and a ploy to solicit attention to one's self. These dynamics will all be explained as we proceed. The fact is—Jeb Bush is not a conservative. Jeb Bush could have used this appearance to speak English; after all, he has stated that all those who enter the country illegally will be required to learn English. This would have been a great opportunity for him to introduce this pledge of his (in English, of course, not Spanish). Then all those listeners would be exposed to an English lesson, maybe some for the very first time, serving to expedite their learning of the language. Does he not mean what he says? The problem is, Jeb Bush is a chameleon, he claims to be a conservative Republican but can be both a RINO, and a CINO.

Although these three individuals are registered Republicans and may self-identify as conservatives, on many occasions and on some specific issues, you would be hard pressed to separate what they say or do from that of a strict liberal position! Hence, we not only call them RINOs; but they qualify as a CINO, which as you just learned is Conservative in Name Only.

We must realize that there is a continuum that may be observed on a scale of severity of the disorder, as we strive to come to an understanding of this affliction called liberalism. This is not an all-or-none proposition. Hence, those lesser affected with liberalism—not realizing the extent of their affliction—may drift into a state of denial. Many may be afflicted with liberalism and not realize it!

But at some point, we've got to cut to the chase and lay the following proposition directly on the table so we can begin to build the structure upon which liberalism the mental and/or psychological disorder may be based.

Keep in mind, as mentioned earlier that the individual is composed of a four quadrant system or call it a four component system. When these four quadrants are working together in complete harmony and rhythm, the individual may indeed experience optimal harmony in the daily functioning of their life and existence. The operation of reason and logic will be a daily component of their life and experience. But when disharmonies begin to dominate and create disruptions in the lives and behavior of many, it is time to stop and evaluate circumstances. It is time for a reality check.

Remember Ross Perot back in 1992, when he made his bid to run in the presidential election? He said, "We're going to pop the hood." His metaphor symbolized taking an analytical look at our nation. Perot used the *popping the hood* metaphor to simulate looking at the state of the nation and economy—and then, to continue the metaphor, check out how this vehicle is running. Continuing, Perot said, "Once we figure out what's wrong with it—we can set about to fix it." Perot, being a practical and common-sense sort of guy, rather than watch the car clank and sputter down the road creating endless havoc and then debating, theorizing, and discussing endlessly from a distance what the problem is, chose rather to go hands on to explore the problem. Perot had in mind to apply the same strategy to an analysis of the state of the nation. We, in the space of this book, are going to do the same thing with the individual. Whatever is analogous to popping the hood. We will pop the psychological hood of the individual and take a look to determine what the problem is.

Of key necessity to arrive at an answer to the causes and etiology of liberalism, we lay the following proposition or hypothesis directly on the table: When it comes to decision making, positions on issues, individual beliefs and attitudes, goals and motivation, factors that govern behavior, et cetera, the one camp, the liberals, are primarily grounded in their emotional quadrant—it is there from whence their decisions, a great deal of their "thinking", and also their beliefs in large part are influenced and proceed.

Contrast that orientation with those of the opposite camp—for now, let's give them the full benefit of a doubt, that they have earned inclusion into the domain of the conservative camp and generously apply the general definition of 'conservative' to them—and call them conservatives (and do not automatically assume they are Republicans). The decision-making process of the conservatives is grounded in their intellectual quadrant. It is in the intellectual quadrant that all sorts of facts, data, information, and statistical analysis are stored, processed, and evaluated—and therefore conclusions rendered.

It is here that we can begin to lay the proper foundation for an understanding of the factors that govern the predisposition towards liberalism, which in turn will further lead us to grasp the essence of the problem. The emotional quadrant is not designed for decision making or logic. Liberals are wrongly (and often times unconsciously) employing the emotional quadrant to do the work naturally designed by God our creator to be done by the intellectual quadrant. For that matter, any work demanded of any one of the four quadrants, the nature of such work the quadrant was not designed to do, can only result in poor decision making and maladapted behavior, which will lead to wrong, if not totally disastrous results consequential to many.

There is so much wrapped up in this one simple proposition, but let's not get enticed into the belief that complex behavior—such as what we see displayed by the liberal—automatically demands a complex answer to understand it.

Let's look at this very simply so we can grasp an understanding of how a human personality quadrant may be employed to do work for which it was designed and nature intended.

In practically any endeavor in life—when all four of the personality quadrants are working in unison and harmony, and each component fulfills the task for which it was ordained by our creator, positive outcomes may be achieved. For now, forget anything you learned about the Freudian id, ego, superego, anal retentive, and all the other catchphrases that have established themselves in the popular lexicon with both the professional and the lay person. They have no bearing whatsoever on what we're discussing nor will they further our understanding.

For example, let's say that Mr. Jones is about to embark on his gardening project, which he has spent a lot of time meticulously planning for. It is time for the garden vegetables and the crops to be planted. Does Mr. Jones casually lounge around thinking about this project for days on end, sitting back in his easy chair imagining how it will "feel" once it's done? Or wishing, by some stroke of luck that God, his spiritual

Father, will magically, physically, and materially make the garden appear at some futuristic time—or for those who reject a spiritual foundation, waiting for the god of entitlement, a.k.a., the government, to produce it for him? Or, as often happens, expect the government to pay him to not produce it. Then, he takes the government handout check to the nearby market to purchase inferior-quality imported goods?

No, of course not. What he does is this. He gets off his ass and engages his physical quadrant to carry out all the necessary mechanical physical tasks! Of course, a great deal of physical work needs to be engaged in to do this task—spading, digging, and tilling, et cetera.

No doubt, all the quadrants from the four quadrant structure of his—all of which are part of his total makeup—are involved in this process—each one to the extent of augmenting and supporting the physical quadrant and each one supporting the other!

Yes, he does engage his thinking quadrant as he formulates and plans how to bring about the synchronization of all the different elements of the project; how to lay out the rows and the number of plants in each row, nurturing each seed he plants to assure its survival, staying up to date with weather and temperature forecasts, the kind of fertilizer to use, and organizing his schedule of care for the plants.

Yes, Mr. Jones does engage his various emotions; ask any farmer or gardener and they will tell you of the strong bond of love that exists between themselves and the soil. George Washington was, first of all, a farmer, as were a majority of our Founding Fathers, and Washington often expressed his intense love for the soil. Further emotional bonds of love are created from the socializing factor whereby family, neighbors, and friends are drawn into the project; all looking forward to contributing to the formation process, as well as partaking of the enjoyment and bounty of the final outcome.

The emotion of jealousy (and don't be thrown off course by this word as we will later on fully explain the meaning of the word as it pertains to the emotion) and zeal stimulates the passion and the drive to vigorously go about his work. Mr. Jones is able to visualize in his mind's eye the bounty and reward of the final outcome of all his laboring which daily motivates him to achieve that end. Each and every morning he awakens early and is up and about by sunrise to tend to his business. He can barely contain his excitement, eager to take on the various tasks!

Finally, engaging his spiritual quadrant, he gives thanks to God his spiritual foundation for providing his abilities and all the resources to carry out this task and asks that his efforts be blessed with bountiful fruit in due season! And once the final outcome is achieved, what a great reward it is! Anyone who has experienced the final bounty of these various stages of labor is well aware of the joy and fulfillment, just as George Washington did. Nowhere is there any sense or notion that he is entitled to enjoy the fruits of this earth without first putting forth sufficient effort to earn them. Earning the benefits of them make them extra special. Only then, may he rightfully proclaim with the utmost of pride, "Yes, with

God's help and not the help of government—I did build that!"

I hope it is clear in the preceding example that all quadrants working in unison and harmony are necessary for goal achievement. If there is an imbalance, disharmony, a lack of any of the various components, or if the state demands possession of the crops with the intent to distribute them among the masses in the name of socialistic *fairness*, then the entire structure upon which the notion of individual initiative rests is weakened, and outcomes may be adversely affected.

CHAPTER 2

EMOTION VS. INTELLECT AND REASON

I t is not sufficient simply to say that liberalism is a mental disorder, and then as if these few words explain the phenomena, unabatedly drift into one of our sleep-states of passivity and conclude, *Great, now that we all fully understand what this means, we need not trouble ourselves any further about it.*

Some talk show hosts and political commentators actually do a decent job of exploring liberalism and discussing the consequences of the proliferation of liberalism; that is, how the disruptive and transformative interventions, and the unrestrained modifications in so many spheres of human activity by the liberals and progressives are leveled against the many traditional institutions of our culture, whether they are governmental, educational, social, or religious; all in the name of rightness, fairness, doing what's best for the individual, governmental guarantees of rights (they ignore the fact that many of the individual rights are inalienable rights granted first by our creator, not to be superimposed upon us by the government), et cetera.

But the dynamics responsible for the specific activities of liberalism, that is, how one's thinking, psychological development, and especially the basic human emotions (as we directed attention to earlier as a prime causative factor) and how all these components together drive and direct the many aspects of the liberal's behavior, is often lacking in the discussion.

If it is a fact that the basic human emotions—and in the circumstance of the liberal mindset are one of the primary factors affecting decisions and outcomes, then it seems expedient that this notion be fully explored. It is necessary to take the discussion to the level of penetrating to the essence and understanding of the human emotions on an esoteric level; and then naming and defining the basic human emotions and how each one of them manifest in the day to day behavior of each and every individual, and for all of one's current life experience considerations; irrespective of the expressed political or social leanings of the individual.

The emotional structure has been a naturally occurring component of the human species, firmly grounded in the instinctual nature of all mankind—for all we know—since the time that man (Homo sapiens) had that first awareness of, "I am" consciousness. And if not originating from that antiquity of time, because it becomes difficult to prove; then it certainly originated from the early Greeks onward, famous for their many passion plays and tragedies which we are aware of passing down to us through historical tradition. Passion, by the way, is another name for emotion. But when we say passion, which emotion(s) are we speaking of? We'll thoroughly explore that as we move forward.

As in the example of the gardener planting the crops, generally speaking, in human activity, all four personality components need to be engaged. What about those circumstances in which the personality components are not working in sync and harmony, augmenting and reinforcing outcomes? What are the consequences if the human emotions are not allowed to manifest in a natural manner? We will discover that the consequence of such disruptions of the natural expression of the emotions is the establishment of the predisposition to extreme liberal behavior and liberalism.

May we at least take it as a working hypothesis that the primary locus of control and activity of the liberal is grounded in their emotional quadrant; and that of the conservative, is grounded in their intellectual quadrant? And don't jump to any conclusion from this that the conservative is without any ability to feel or the liberal is without any ability to think. As said earlier, it is a condition of degree.

Those on the conservative side of the spectrum who have the ability to fully engage their intellect—free of emotional bias and irrational beliefs, would express that the answer to so many of the severely contentious issues argued on the national stage—have, what anyone in their right mind would say, is a clearly recognizable obvious answer—the answer to certain issues of which may be based upon pure reason—a product of the head-brain and intellect. And a very close ally of reason is logic, again, a product of the head-brain and intellect. And following that is another close ally of the two—that is, *common sense*! All have undoubtedly heard it said, "All it takes is some common sense to understand that."

Common sense is also derived from the head-brain, as common sense incorporates logic and reason, tempered by experience—oftentimes, experience consistently replicated. Common sense has nothing to do with emotional functioning. The irony of the phrase common sense is that the word *common,* denoting something universal and widely shared—as it turns out, it may not be as common as everyone thinks!

But there is this curious perception of common sense. Is it just me who has this perception, or do you have this perception as well, that common sense is a product more associated with; the uneducated, the unwashed masses, those who dwell in flyover country, and those who rely on their guns and religion? Those individuals just described are sometimes referred to pejoratively as "country people" as if they are lacking in sophistication. But it doesn't mean they are lacking in intelligence just because they are not urbanites, Ivy Leaguers, or east coast elitists. These same "country people" often use that term when referencing leadership in far off Washington, asking why they can't demonstrate more common sense. But then again, this term may be used by many across America, regardless of their station or class. Has this term become associated with lack of sophistication and even shunned by those in Washington due to the association of it with a powerful voice heard at the time of our nation's founding—the words of Thomas Paine?

Thomas Paine, as you may recall from history, at the founding of our nation was a big proponent of common sense. It was on the foundation of using common sense that Paine launched his attacks against the oppressiveness of the British Crown and against big government(s) in general. How does it happen that common sense played a big role at the formation of our country, but nowadays the employment of it seems to be totally lacking on Capitol Hill and in the media. Perhaps the notion that our ills may be cured by infusing some common sense strikes a bit too close to home for the entrenched big-government Washington bureaucrats and is seen as a threat to their power. Has Thomas Paine become a victim of revisionist history along with his associated common sense—as it is a fact that the liberals love to attack our Founding Fathers, and attack the Constitution, which to them is viewed as a living malleable document, and for the most part outdated?

The late conservative William F. Buckley said, "There is a better chance of a repository of the kind of wisdom I choose to be governed by among average people than among PhDs at Harvard."[2] Is common sense normally associated with or is it used less by Washington elitists, many of whom are former Ivy Leaguers? Do you get a sense that it is beneath them? And even when one of our elected officials refers to the obvious benefits of common sense, it doesn't seem to get much traction.

The use of common sense is not a factor when it comes to the passage of laws in the halls of Congress or the Senate. If it had been a factor, then the Democrats who unanimously passed Obamacare would perhaps have realized that the government would screw up healthcare in the same manner it screwed up Amtrak, the Postal Service, veteran's health care, or any other endeavor it gets its hands in. It also seems a very practical matter, even common sense, that the 2,700-page *Affordable Care Act* would be thoroughly read and reviewed by everyone in the Senate, House, and by President Obama before submitting a vote on it, passing it, and signing it.

Is there any reason or logic to the statement of Nancy Pelosi, when referring to the *Affordable Care Act*, "We need to pass it so we can find out what's in it"? All the while the American people were screaming at the top of their lungs, "Don't you think you need to read it first?" But it was important to pass Obamacare because it felt good (and this of course was not the only reason to pass the bill)! Now we are all supposed to feel good that everyone has health care! The question to all those who voted for the Obamacare: From which major emotion did you draw to make your decision to pass the bill? This question may be difficult to answer at the moment because we have not at this point delineated the primary emotions. What happened to reason, logic, and common sense?

Here's another problem where the application of common sense is lacking: regarding the illegal entry of people carried on at our borders. If we really want to fix the illegal immigration problem, why not first protect and seal the border? Is that not one of the first steps in a common sense approach? But Washington does NOT want to do that! They shun common sense! But then, too, they have other selfish interests and motivations at heart that prevent them from making that decision.

This is a fact: the emotional quadrant of an individual possesses no logic, no reason, nor common sense. It was not designed to do that and never will be! But yet, so very much of what we see instituted in our nation is constructed upon this faulty foundation, which is founded upon emotionalism, which generally goes hand in hand with its by-product and producing disastrous unintended consequences, which is, out of control liberalism! Recall how often you hear someone on Capitol Hill say, "I will vote for this bill because I feel very strongly about it!"

Really! But did you read it and study it thoroughly and then tediously study all the various ramifications of it applicable to not only the present, but the future impact of it? Did you measure and carefully weigh all the various ramifications of it that may affect the citizens personally, financially, and for all posterity? Explain to all of your constituents, please, how can one feel a bill?

There exist countless examples to demonstrate and prove my point of how the emotional quadrant is wrongly employed to do the work of the intellectual quadrant, but for now I'll give you just this one following example.

Regarding the recent Muslim-inspired attack on *Charlie Hebdo* in Paris, Eugene Robinson of the *Washington Post* was reported to have said he was so glad that didn't happen here [in the USA]. "Just to keep it into perspective, I don't think we should imagine that the conditions and the threat are exactly the same in the United States as they are in France. They are different. In fact, one thing that is different here is weapons are universally available and so it is actually a very good thing that, that the tensions are not exactly the same because we would expect to have a lot more carnage because those gun nuts would have made it much worse."[1]

In this one example, in my opinion, there is absolutely no reason, facts, nor logic upon which to base such a ridiculous wrong-headed statement! This is a response based upon raw unrestrained emotion. Would such a statement be made out of a framework of sound reasoning and logic? I would say no! And the primary emotional foundation supporting such a statement is the specific emotion of fear—but fear of what? What is Mr. Robinson afraid of? Was it a fear of guns which are innately inanimate instruments, or was it fear of certain people who have in their hands a gun? What will those gun nuts do that he very much fears? What is the foundation of your statement? We all challenge you to step forth and come up with plausible answers, Mr. Robinson! I don't believe Mr. Robinson went on to explain himself. Perhaps he himself is unaware of what his motivation is to say such a thing—as generally these emotion-driven knee-jerk reactionary statements proceed from one's unconscious fanaticism-driven motivations of which the person has no conscious awareness. He may be fixated upon a notion that it would 'feel' so good if no guns existed in the world! I'm just guessing and speculating. What do you think?

Then, across our nation, all those people who hear these ridiculous statements of his; they, in a like fashion who internalize within themselves various repressions of fear which is ingrained and repressed in their very own psyche in like manner as in Mr. Robinson's, will identify and glom on to them. They will get on the same bandwagon and join Mr. Robinson with the same brand of ranting and outrage, never stopping to reflect upon the position they take on the issue nor their motivation supporting it—as the basis supporting it is blind fanatical belief driven by unconscious motivations. And as their numbers increase, the magnitude of their insanity is directly proportional to the increase of their numbers. Progressively, rational thinking and critical thinking are blotted out and they all settle into the comforting enclave provided by this mass conformity such as we see in a massive collection of ocean herring, all gathering together as if their mass creates a façade of strength.[1]

The greater the numbers of people grow—the deeper they all sink into this hypnotic dream-state, their eyes becoming glazed over and their actions then becoming even more mechanical and unconscious. And the justifications and argued rationale for their behaviors

---

[1] *It should be noted that the emotion of fear when looked at across the spectrum of many different individuals... many may not necessarily have the same original unconscious source associated with it as with that individual (in this instance, Mr. Robinson) with whom they are identified. Fear is an equal opportunity intruder and this emotion will hijack any life situation and attach unto it—wherever it can get an edge to vent and expel any repressed emotion from within an individual's unconscious. The object of the projection does not matter so much as the task of the unconscious attempting to achieve balance in the psyche by expelling the poison of the repressed emotion (in this case fear)... but more about this later in the chapter on fear.)*

are shifted away from the individual and transferred to the sheer numbers of the collective, relieving the individual of any responsibility while at the same time giving the collective a false sense that they really now belong to something worthwhile and special.

Those are the ones of like character and behavioral propensities who will join the chorus—who will begin to angrily shout out the one-line slogans, such as, "No Justice—No Peace!" "We Want Environmental Justice Now!" "Bush lied—People died" "Social Justice for All" "Hands Up—Don't Shoot" "Black Lives Matter" "Frying Like Bacon, Pigs in a Blanket" or some other such vacuously brainless slogan, the wording of which is modeled to fit the circumstance, even with no logical association or at best, only loosely associated with it!

Do you remember your physics classes in school in which your instructor conducted an exercise in striking tuning forks? The instructor struck a tuning fork and the tuning fork held by the student(s) across the room—constructed according to the laws of physics and mechanics—would respond to and then emit the same rate of vibration as if in orchestrated unison.

Regarding all those who automatically succumb to the chorus of these brainless one-liners, metaphorically, they are like all of those like-constructed tuning forks constructed to succumb to and then emit the same rate of vibration... in this case, the same kind of behavior. Just like those tuning forks that when struck—as those waves pass through the atmosphere—will trigger the same rate of vibration in like constructed tuning forks wherever they may be.

In this instance, people are like those tuning forks—the susceptible masses all resonate together as one, all emitting duplicate behavior patterns, whether dwelling in the cities or across the fruited plain of our country. Here, in the classroom, it is a physical phenomena, but in the transmission of the energy among humans it becomes both a physical and a psychic phenomena. Collectively, they too carry the same sort of repressions and attitudes within their psyche and therefore all resonate together as one. In this scenario— all identities are absorbed into the masses and each ceases to exist as an individual. And the price they pay for the brief superficial comfort of temporarily 'belonging' to the herd is the cost incurred by the sacrifice of the experience of genuine individuality and freedom.

CHAPTER 3

LIBERALISM: A PSYCHIC EMOTIONAL DEVELOPMENTAL DISORDER

I t is of necessity in the field of mental health that an official nomenclature is needed for the identification of various mental disorders. Periodically the need arises to introduce and coin new terms for the purpose of naming a condition. This has actually gone on for decades and generally proceeds when psychic and behavioral conditions of humanity reach a certain height of activity and regularity in their occurrence. There could not be a better time for the introduction of a new diagnostic term as the propensity to liberal behavior has reached a fever pitch. For the purpose of describing what has become commonly recognized as liberalism—the mental disorder—there should be no doubt that the term currently in use, offers nothing that comes close to fully explaining the condition of liberalism. Therefore, the new term I will introduce is Psychic Emotional Developmental Disorder (PEDD).

Let's take this new term and break it down.

Indeed, liberalism is a disorder encompassing the individual's psyche, and the individual's emotions play a dominant role in the formation and the etiology of the condition. The initial onset period occurs during the individual's early development, and in fact with the passage of time the cumulative compounded repetition results in an acquired disorder ... a condition which may unfortunately remain with the individual for a lifetime, unless that person immerse himself or herself in critical, unbiased, and relentless self-examination, with the aim to purge themselves of all the factors creating this horrible curse.

To fully understand liberalism, one must go beyond simply putting a name to it. Hence, I want to further expand on the etiology of the condition.

The primary foundation of the disorder PEDD rests in great part upon the emotional component of the human species. This component serves as the primary foundation from which the disorder called liberalism, the mental disorder, manifests. Understanding that the emotions are the primary foundation and the driving forces of this condition, it is equally important to understand how the emotions interface with the mental (brain) component. After all, thinking is a function of the brain and feeling is a function of the emotions, and there should be no allowance for any confusion when identifying liberal behavior as a mental disorder.

After decades of the evolution—that is, of the study, classifications, and observations of the paradigm of mental health in our country—it seems reasonable that we would have a better grasp of the location, classification, and role of the emotions, but I don't believe we've come sufficiently far in our understanding of that very important component. Perhaps this is due to too much emphasis on the mental when attempting to sort out psychological disorders. We have been too quick to retreat to using the term *mental illness.*

The domicile of the emotions is not in the head or brain, although often one may feel that they are. For example, when someone goes into a blind rage of anger—which surely is the peak of experience of the discharge of anger—all reason and logic (assuming there was some present to begin with) is suspended, and that person so engaged in anger may feel their head will burst and all awareness is blotted out. That's why it's called a blind rage. Rationality ceases! Surely, many of you may have witnessed such phenomena. It just so happens that contemporaneous with the writing of this book reports are again resurfacing in various media of how Hillary Clinton, in a rage-filled discharge of anger, literally physically wounded Bill Clinton in a bloody mêlée in the White House—reportedly throwing a lamp (or book?) or whatever the object was, directly at him![1] Presumably, she only then learned of the affair with Monica Lewinsky.

Now, ladies and gentlemen, do you believe that in this household encounter, assuming it happened (and we really may not know all the specific facts of what happened) that there was any semblance of proportionality to the extent that Hillary responded to an act committed by Bill, which he committed in that very close time frame … was perhaps, just an innocent little bedroom argument? No, of course not!

What's absent in this phenomena is the element of proportionality, and those of you who have witnessed such a rage-filled episode—or perhaps it has happened to you—these rage-filled expressions and displays far exceed a balanced reaction to the circumstances which occurred in that exact time frame. The act by Bill would have had to be something of a great magnitude to generate such a response from Hillary. We can only speculate what it could have been.

In my opinion Hillary displayed what is generally displayed in such a vehement explosion as this: the sudden discharge and release of a festering pool of anger, hatred, and hostility which has accumulated over a period of time. A key question that needs to be answered when addressing these kinds of emotional discharges then becomes, is that festering pool completely drained of all the hate-filled repressions?

An even more challenging question to ask is, when did the formation of these festering pools of anger have their initial onset? Generally, such conditions as this require an individual to commit to critical and unbiased introspection to uncover the initial onset event(s). Another key question to be asked is, does Hillary still have the predisposition to lose her head in a given situation—effectively suspending all reason and logic?

Depending on the answer to these two questions, the electorate needs to evaluate whether or not we want her holding political office. Do you believe that this one venting episode against Bill discharged all of her pent up anger? What do you think?

Of importance is whether or not there is a certain regularity or periodicity in the venting of anger in intermittent magnitudes of displays. This is what is commonly described as one periodically being in a state of having a temper, being hot tempered, temperamental, or one predisposed to losing control. Those who are regularly predisposed to having a temper, have at the core of their unconscious some repressions of anger which never get full resolution, and the longer these repressions of anger fester and multiply, they will likely turn into a pool of hatred.

Additionally, as a reinforcement and a conditioning factor that supports the behavior patterns of the hot-tempered person, they learn (and they also learn to perceive it to be to their advantage) that many people fear anger and will cower in the midst of its expression, and because of that, the hot-tempered person learns to use the intense expression of anger as a tool to control and manipulate those same cowardly people in order to achieve their objective. Furthermore, they may get a sadistic enjoyment from controlling those individuals, and in the end, getting it done *my way*. It's my way, or the highway!

It is a curious phenomenon in our society that many individuals do fear anger. There is no denying that there exists a perception that the general public views anger in a negative manner, as a bad thing. These views and beliefs have become rooted in the psyche of many Americans and are passed on from one generation to the next, mostly by the adults through their words and actions influencing the impressionable young, who learn by observing and then mimicking those behaviors. These beliefs form the basis of those perpetual attitudes towards anger. When a person fears anger, they are reticent to express it, or may cower when in the midst of the expression of it.

Hence, when these intense displays of anger happen, the presiding authorities, public or private human resource departments, or mental health providers, will direct that hot-tempered person to anger management to assist the out-of-control person to control their anger—or in extreme cases, haul them off to jail for committing assault or breaking a law.

Has it ever been suggested to Hillary that she enroll in some anger management intervention? Regarding the Benghazi attack hearings in Congress, if Hillary had uttered the words, "What difference does it make" in the same shrill, angry fashion within the confines of a private corporate America setting as she did on the floor of the House, she would have been escorted to visit the human resources department and henceforth mandated to partake of anger management intervention.

In such extreme circumstances, it becomes very clear that the emotions are the primary drivers of behavior, as in the example of the Clinton's just provided. Anger was the driver of Hillary's behavior. What's the line from that famous poem of Rudyard Kipling, "If you can keep your head when all about you are losing theirs and blaming it on you ... "[2] Is it even possible to visualize Hillary in a calm, balanced, voice and manner saying, "Yes, Bill you bastard, it is your entire fault!" Could she do that without having to throw objects at him? No, because too much anger had been festering and gathering, ready to erupt.

During an extreme infusion of emotion—as the anger intrudes into the head and brain activity—sane thinking, reason, and logic are all suspended and adversely affected, generally resulting in poor decision making and outcomes of behavior in those circumstances. And what has to be understood is that in these circumstances, this is an extrusion of repressed emotion breaking forth from the unconscious of the person and intruding forcefully into the brain and thinking activity, and not necessarily exclusively in a proportional reaction to the present circumstance. If one expresses anger that is in direct proportion to the circumstance, there is no risk, or certainly little risk that one will lose their head.

And to be clear, this autonomous infusion of emotion into the brain need not be limited to the emotion of anger alone, but different behaviors may present with other specific primary emotions serving as the drivers of that behavior. And if the emotions proceed from a repressed pool, then the result is generally a lack of proportionality in the expression of it in the context of the present moment, and again, consequently, the brain and thinking will be affected.

According to medical science, we know that there is an organic physiological interface between the brain and the emotions. There exist neurotransmitters which relay emotional signals to the brain. Various kinds of drugs were invented that, when administered, would inhibit or enhance the chemistry of the neurotransmitters. Then, when an individual was diagnosed with mood or affective (feeling) disorders, the purpose of the drugs were to suppress and inhibit emotion—with the end goal to stabilize the emotions. But keep in mind that drug treatment, sadly and unfortunately, is only addressing symptoms and do not go to the heart of repairing the emotional disorder. That, in my opinion is a misfortune.

Regarding the DSM-5, though intended to serve as an all-purpose reference manual for the classification of mental disorders; still, after all these revisions, it does not classify emotional disorders, per se.[3] You will not find this term of mine, PEDD, presented in the DSM-5 because I just came up with it. Perhaps one day such a diagnosis will be added to a future DSM revision, but don't count on it as long as the task force of the DSM is strongly influenced and politicized by liberals. I believe this new term is quite suitable for the DSM. It just sort of synchronizes with the general rhythm of the lexicon. Go ahead, if you're curious and you have the time—pick up a copy of the DSM and read it so you can learn more about it!

The DSM devotes a sizable portion of its content to "Mood Disorders" and "Affective Disorders". But I do not believe the DSM ever refers to an emotional disorder by the strict use of just those words! As a matter of fact, one would be hard pressed to find much usage of the word *emotions* mentioned in the DSM at all! Words such as *depression, anxious, sad, depressed, in a bad mood,* et cetera, are used. But the primary emotions, of which each person is blessed with at birth, are given scant attention in the DSM and certainly not in the terms and classifications used!

Nowhere in academia, nowhere in the preparatory curriculum of the major colleges and universities, nowhere in the curriculum aimed at preparing students for a profession in the mental health setting, is there found an exact cataloging of the *primary human emotions*; certainly not as you'll see presented in this book. What are they? You may Google and Nexus-Lexus the phrase primary human emotions until you're blue in the face, but you will not find any sources that are in sync with the aim to accurately identify them. If you doubt me, tweet Dr. Charles Krauthammer of FOX News. He's a very bright man, schooled and trained in psychiatry, and I'm sure he's very familiar with what's in academia as well as the various DSM renditions. Perhaps he can give you some feedback. There is not even a general consensus of what the primary human emotions are, assuming that a consensus even offers any strength to the validity of the cataloging.

But beware of consensus. After all, consensus is one of the building blocks. It begins to lay the foundation and is just a step away from creating the dangerous condition of herd conformity and groupthink. Even the most brilliant minds in our country may become subject to the enticement of herd conformity. I guess it has to do with one feeling safer when immersed within large numbers. Also, in a way, it relieves the individual of having to stand alone on an issue and to take responsibility for something and bear the full onslaught of criticism of something, should they be assaulted by the masses. If wrong, the group takes the hit. I am sheltered in the safe enclave of my consensus group.

If my new classification, PEDD, should ever find its way into the DSM—under the auspices of the *Affordable Care Act*, regarding the enrollment and coverage guidelines, and insurance allowable treatment cost—will liberalism fall under the category of a pre-existing condition so that full, low-cost treatment coverage may be obtained to treat the condition of liberalism?[5]

CHAPTER 4

MORE ABOUT THINKING AND FEELING

It has been said that Homo sapiens are creatures of habit in the respect that exemplified in their behavior and true to their nature are repetitive patterns and ritualistic forms of activity, whether these patterns are displayed in speech or actions. Patterns of actions and behaviors become steadfastly ingrained in many of our activities, and once ingrained, that behavior may be carried out quite automatically and without much conscious thought, if any. Such is the case in what I now need to make a point of order about. You've heard of the 10 Times Rule, haven't you? If you want to form a habit, you perform the behavior ten times and then the behavior becomes ingrained at an unconscious level and henceforth is carried out automatically, unconsciously.

But in employing the 10 Times Rule, we generally set a goal, do a specific task, and after ten repetitions of performing that task, it becomes a habit. Behaviors may also become ingrained without our conscious intent to carry them out, but simply because we observe and mimic behaviors.

In the general exchanges of vocabulary and in conversation of individuals across the country—and this includes liberals, conservatives, whoever—there occurs a very automatic and unconscious, if not downright careless usage of the words *feeling* and *feel*. I assume that people are talking about the human emotions when they say they feel such and such or have a feeling about this, that, or the other. But are they? When the words *feeling* and *feel* are used so indiscriminately, is reference being made exclusively to the human emotional component?

In conversation someone may say, "Oh, I feel such and such. I feel that so and so," and so on. Or, "I have a feeling that … " Very often one may say, "I feel this … " when in reality, in analyzing the content and context of their conversation, they should rather be describing an activity of functioning proceeding from their thinking quadrant or maybe even describing a belief or a perception coming from the sphere of the intuitive (spiritual) quadrant of their personality. Humans do have that capacity to perceive via a sixth sense that proceeds from their intuitive (spiritual) quadrant. Hence, something proceeding from that quadrant would be identified by the individual as an intuitive feeling.

But even in that circumstance, is it accurate to say, "I have a feeling"? Rather, is it not better termed to describe it as an intuitive perception or intuitive hunch and not to be termed a feeling or emotion as if proceeding from the emotional quadrant? Emotion and intuition is not the same thing.

Is it possible that when individuals are referring to feelings when they say, "I feel such and such," there may be no connection whatsoever with the emotions? If I were to place a wager on the proposition that liberals are more likely to use the word feel in various conversations than do conservatives, then yes, I place my bets on liberals! Remember, liberals are more likely to feel their way through life because their central control and much of their thinking proceed from their emotions.

Then, making the waters even muddier, someone may use the word *feel* or *feeling* to define the position of the group or collective, such as, "We feel," or the congressman proclaiming after the convening and findings of their special committee, "We strongly feel that ... " Now even a group or committee suddenly has an emotional foundation that is shared by the collective. How on earth can a committee feel? A committee cannot feel. The job of a committee is to come up with facts, logic, and a workable, mutually beneficial plan in accordance with whatever they are focused upon.

Recently on a Sunday morning news hour, a congressman was expressing comments regarding a hot news item. As I recall, it had to do with the proposed Iran and American nuclear proliferation agreement. Regarding this particular committee to which he belonged, he said, "We all feel regarding this issue..." Whether it's this particular issue or any other, it is important to note that a group or committee cannot feel. What did the committee chairperson do, take a poll of the committee members to determine how each one felt? Only a person has the capacity and the ability to feel, and then via the emotional quadrant.

Furthermore, if the best this committee can come up with is a feeling, then it seems appropriate that the voters question what this committee is up to. What about their individual abilities and how their abilities create focus, strategies, and goals for the committee? These people are the elected leadership, you may recall, and we the people should expect more of them. Do they know what they're doing? Is the best that they can muster of their abilities limited to making decisions that profoundly affect us all based upon a feeling?

Congressional committees are not the only elected officials who resort to basing strategies upon feelings. Bill Clinton made the quote famous by his repetition when, with quivering lip, he said, "I feel your pain." Do you remember that? No doubt he used this line many times. It was a real vote-getter! Surely, many thought, "Now here is a man who truly understands and furthermore understands by feeling. He knows exactly how you feel, don't you think?" The liberal media and many voters bought into this nonsense. Bill Clinton was intent on proving he had genuine compassion (feeling). And make no mistake about it, liberals believe they alone have the ability to have compassion and only they can genuinely feel.

But for Bill to claim he can feel someone else's pain is impossible. The only pain Bill may feel is his own. The only physical pain Bill may feel is his own, such as when Hillary hurled that book or lamp or whatever it was at him in the White House bedroom. It is impossible for Bill to feel someone else's pain. It is impossible for me to feel your pain. It is impossible for you to feel my pain. Only I can feel my pain or whichever emotion happens to be at the fore.

And then, are we talking about physical pain or emotional pain? Even to say to someone in pain, "I understand what you're going through" is a stretch. We never absolutely know precisely what the other person is going through because the experience of each and every individual is unique to that very individual. Indeed we may have experienced something we believe is similar to what the person we're extending compassion to may be experiencing. The best and most accurate thing we may do is to extend our empathy and love, but liberals believe they have this special capacity that allows them to feel anyone's pain because of the fact that they see themselves as such feeling people, and therefore, the liberals are going to rid you of your pain and fear, because they know exactly what you're going through, and they know much better than you what's best for you!

So now, Mr. or Mrs. True Conservative, when you meet up with someone like this you can be assured you are dealing with a liberal.

Liberals believe they have this uncanny ability to experience the pain of anyone, even to the extent of crossing the long-past time boundary back to generations of those long gone. Every now and then, a liberal in Congress or leadership revives the need to push for current reparations to reward and compensate black Americans alive today, to help them ease the pain they feel for the institution of slavery in America.

The fact is, there is not one black American alive today who experienced slavery in America. It is impossible for any currently living black person to know that experience of slavery, unless somehow they were captured by a hostile nation—today!—and sold into slavery; but even that experience would not duplicate the exclusively American experience of slavery! Generally, the true motive behind these rather shoddy altruistic endeavors is to get the vote of the black Americans, a campaign strategy staged by the liberals.

Very often and very prevalent in our culture there is a very high premium placed upon feeling. Have you noticed that? If someone says, "I feel such and such ... ,"everyone gets in a tizzy and says, "Wow, so and so feels!" But then if you disagree with their basic premise, you may be subject to some severe criticism and reprimand. How do you counter and argue against what someone feels? You can't! They will respond, "But that's how I feel"!

The truth is, if the word *feel* were replaced by the word *think* in the very same context and sentence one utters, and the circumstance they are describing remained exactly the same, regardless, in the understanding of the various listeners' perception, there would then be a difference, just by switching the use of that one word, *feel* to *think*!

A feeling can be so highly subjective. It's difficult to counter subjectivity; it becomes like gospel, even though, no one knows what the feelings' are anyway! And here we're talking of real feelings stemming from the primary emotions. There has been no clearly defined cataloging of feelings; that is, the primary human emotions. This how I feel position (and they are sticking to it because that's how they feel) is supported by the view that has come into vogue during the last few decades which embodies this notion that everyone is entitled to their own truth. The liberals believe everyone's truth must be respected, even if it comes into direct opposition to longstanding, time-honored, universal laws and truth. One's own truth is incontestable, even when subject to scrutiny and weighed against any longstanding irrevocable laws or stacked against sound reason and logic.

It's as if in our modern culture objectivity is turned on its head and subjectivity rules the day! Objectivity is more closely associated with the thinking and the intellect. Subjectivity is more closely associated with the emotions.

Liberals and liberalism abhor universal, perennial, absolute truths. To a liberal, truth is what they feel at any given moment in time and it is incontestable. Whereas, if one says, "I think such and such … " it may become a hotly contested notion (or whatever is expressed). It may be perceived as nothing more than a thought based upon an opinion, even though there may be at least some semblance of pure reason and factual information included in that person's position of opinion. Submitting pure reason and factual information is not enough to counter the feeling of the liberal, for the simple reason that they'll come back at you and say, "I don't care what you say, it doesn't matter—that's how I feel!"

The following is a fine example of what I'm talking about.

David Axelrod's recent book, based upon his memoirs, accused our current president now occupying the White House, Barack Hussein Obama (who you may recall was supported and received in each election cycle roughly 50 to 55 million votes from the citizenry and non-citizenry—voters of whom in a manner were like all those many tuning forks across our land— resonating with the liberal president) of feigning his opposition to gay marriage. Axelrod further stated that for President Barack Hussein Obama to express his true beliefs would hurt him politically in the polls and election outcome coming up in 2012.

President Barack Hussein Obama's defense consisted of accusing Axelrod, quote, "[O]f mixing up my personal feelings with my position on the issue." His feelings of what? Really? Can one's feelings be in opposition to one's thinking, or as Obama said, position, albeit, on the very same issue? What is he talking about? Then, President Barack Hussein Obama opposed it! Or at least he equivocated profusely! Back then, did President Obama think one way; and feel the exact opposite on the very same issue?

What if President Barack Hussein Obama had of said, "Mixing up my personal thinking," then that would have been an admission that Axelrod was correct, and an admission that it was an equivocation and lie by President Obama! And President Barack Hussein Obama would never admit to his lies exposing his pathology. Of course, the liberal media will slice and dice this one every which way to protect both of these liberals. Resting one's argument on feelings allows one to get away with all manner of lies because of the baseless subjectivity.

So then, the same topic may be associated with either feeling or thinking, in which case, at the heart of is still often only an opinion dressed up in the garb of feeling. And opinions (and beliefs, for that matter) run rampant and are subject to endless argument and contestability. Opinions are as ubiquitous as assholes; everyone has at least one. Now, after evaluating the preceding, are you still interested in elevating public opinion polls to any degree of real importance?

Someone who regularly and consistently takes a strong, steadfast stand on various issues in terms of their thought and judgment may be criticized as being opinionated. But on the other hand, a person who feels their way through life may be held in much higher regard because feelings are so sacrosanct! Do you find that to be true?

Often, feeling generally supersedes and trounces thinking in our modern culture. Liberals feel their way through life, and by some twisted quirk, get away with it! And the reason they get away with it ... drawing from the metaphor of the tuning fork mentioned earlier ... all the mindless liberals across the fruited plane, including the great number in the national media, and very many of our elected officials, all resonate so well with it!

Reason is not one of mankind's fully exercised and fully engaged gifts of potential. For very many, reason remains, for the most part, in a latent state and may remain there for one's entire lifetime ... unused and untapped!

You have undoubtedly heard it said, "Man (Homo sapiens) is the only creature of God's creation possessing the gift of reason." The truth is, reason is not a gift as in, "Here it is—take it—it's free for the asking!" Not at all. Rather, it is an acquired and earned trait! For one to engage in pure reason, their thinking must be free of the interference of repressed overriding emotions. For any individual to achieve this task is of Herculean magnitude!

CHAPTER 5

FOUNDATIONS OF THE PRIMARY HUMAN EMOTIONS

Were it not for the primary human emotions, the life experience of the individual would have no zest, no depth, no excitement, no drive to goal-achievement, no positive aggression to challenge obstacles, no passion to spur one forward in the attainment and then support of a cause or belief, no connectedness to other individuals on an intimate, personal, or social level. And for the most part, an individual's life would be without an indispensible implement that is absolutely necessary for one to experience a quality transformative experience in this all too often brief period of their human existence.

The quality of one's lifetime experiences and the positive outcomes aimed for and achieved in life are indispensable underpinnings of human existence. They serve as part of the very building blocks that enable one on this earthly path of spiritual evolution to complete our return back to God from whence we came. On this path of one's individual spiritual evolution—each one of us is faced daily with myriad choices that of necessity we must make; for it is through the experiences gained that we grow, expand our awareness, and increase our being and knowledge as creatures of God. We determine the quality and outcome of those experiences.

The initiating factor and driving force behind all of these choices, without exception, is emotion. One may present the argument and raise the question, "Who says I must of necessity make choices?" Suppose I decide in a certain situation to not make a choice one way or the other? They may say, "So see here, in this instance I made no choice." But then, is this not a side-stepping of the necessity and responsibility of making choices? Even then, in that situation, to make no choice one way or the other is in itself a choice.

Furthermore, in that situation, generally the driving emotion behind this non-choice may be the emotion of fear. Why is it you're afraid of in not making a choice? Is it public opinion, political correctness, fearing to take responsibility for your choice, or fear of criticism? Sometimes our congressmen and senators will carry out a no vote or vote absent in regard to an issue. What's that all about? Are they fearful about voting one way or another? Are they hiding from something? Is this their way of proclaiming, "I am a moderate and choose to ride the fence,"—believing that by some sort of ill-perceived self-righteousness this stance keeps them above the fray?

Sometimes they may believe it's politically expedient of them to make no choice on a vote, but then they're placing their selfish political interests and ambitions above doing the right thing. And that it is a choice they make, and with that choice as with every other choice they make comes accountability.

It is emotion that drives our choices and enables us to take on and surmount challenges, and without myriad choices and challenges—there can be no spiritual evolution. As simply stated in Genesis 3:5, *For God knows that in the day you eat of it, your eyes shall be opened, and you shall be like gods, knowing good and evil.* Knowing good and evil is simply a symbolic representation, a metaphor, of that main ingredient that drives our spiritual evolution. And that main ingredient is the element of *choice* that pervades the existence of each and every individual on this planet!

By exercising and carrying out choices, we open the door to create the opportunities that enable us to gain the wisdom of outcomes of decisions... and in a manner of speaking, 'to know good and evil,' whether the outcome of our choice works toward our betterment or our detriment. Whichever it is, we live with the outcome. This is the recompense we receive for acceptance of responsibility of our choices.

Can you imagine a state of existence in which the element of choice did not exist? Well yes, we can! In the extreme, if we knew precisely the outcome of every decision or event we were involved in—if everything was unequivocally pre-determined in our life—don't you think life would be dull, uninteresting, and boring? Spiritual evolution would come to a stop because there would be no growth. In a manner, then, life would become a perpetual monotony.

Consider the following: The nearest approximation of actually existing in this world of reality just described—that is, of one being deprived of choice—would be an existence in an oppressive totalitarian state! Under such conditions, the state makes your decisions for you. Your so-called choices are limited to what the state demands of you. Your so-called choices are limited to an ever-increasing number of laws, rules, and regulations. Your so-called choices are driven by that hideous cancer that has taken hold in our culture—known by the name of political correctness— the enforcement thereof is in turn driven by one of the most insidious of tools—the high-jacking of and the manipulation of the natural emotion of fear—the emotion that exists within each and every individual.

Is this beginning to sound familiar? Does this not describe the drift of circumstances in the United States of America? It is worth repeating: with no choice, there is no spiritual evolution! With no choice, the human emotions essentially become disengaged and useless. When the human emotions are disengaged, useless, or repressed, we are inhibited from a real experience of our spiritual being, and hence, our journey back to God is thwarted in an environment of coercive statism, authoritarianism, and totalitarianism.

Were it not for the emotional component, we would be like the Coneheads. Do you remember them from the old *Saturday Night Live* program? Their communication tended to be monosyllabic, with a lack of voice inflection revealing a lack of emotional depth or presence. Just as in the life of the Coneheads, life would be monotone were it not for the emotions. The primary emotions working in harmony and rhythm are the drivers of behavior propelling us forward.

The organ of the emotions is located primarily in the solar plexus and extending throughout and along the nerve and spinal ganglia. That is the seat or, it may be said, the brain of the emotions. The emotions are not located in the head, nor are they a part of the gray matter of the brain.

At birth, each and every individual is blessed by their Creator-God with only FIVE ... that's correct, not four, not eight, not 127, such as you may see represented in that long list of feeling words that gets circulated around. Those 127 words (give or take a few) are nothing more than intellectual and semantic constructs that branch off of and are ultimately rooted in the five basic emotions—but only FIVE primary emotions.

Periodically, someone will come up with that long list of feeling words. The list goes on and on, with dozens of words presumably designed to help us determine what we are feeling. You don't need it. You may toss that list in the garbage heap. And while you're at it—toss political correctness in the same garbage heap! You will do both yourself and all humanity a huge favor!

The emotions become engaged and activated very early in the life of the infant and child, as early as six months of age. Even at that young age, the emotions are soon in full working capacity and are well into the process of engaging and speedily becoming fully operational. The brilliance of God our Creator designed us that way. The emotions engage autonomously and function independently of an infant or young child's thought and brain activity, or, in other words, purely from an automatic instinctual unconscious level. The emotions are a separate component. Therefore, it is of utmost importance that the emotional component of each individual is established upon a stable rhythmic foundation.

It may be said that in the scale of highest priority, in terms of the highest worth that contributes to the healthy foundation and formation of the child, the formation of a rhythmic foundation of the emotions are exceeded in value only by the love, care, guidance, and concern of the parents (a mom and a dad) who themselves, it is to be expected, have their own emotional house in order!

The emotions are the primary drivers of human behavior! Regarding the preceding sentence you just read, you must grasp this concept. Please ... stop ... read it again and repeat it to yourself aloud, as this concept is so vitally important to the understanding of human behavior! Do the ten times rule that we talked about earlier. Let's repeat; "The emotions are the PRIMARY DRIVERS of HUMAN BEHAVIOR! Everyone must get this! Recall those times growing up, perhaps in grade school, when the teacher said, "OK, student, go to the blackboard and write this ten times to help you remember it." Dear reader, do that now in your mind's eye. Imagine yourself as a young student walking up to the blackboard, picking up the piece of chalk and writing those words that are capitalized above! Go ahead. Do it now! Imagine those musky smells of that classroom intermixed with a lingering smell of chalk dust in the air as you dutifully write each line. Recall the muffled squeak of the chalk as it roughly glides across the board. If you take nothing else away from the reading of this book, it is my hope that you at least internalize and understand these very important concepts of the human emotions.

To help you to grasp this concept, begin today to observe yourself and observe others on a daily basis and you will begin to identify and understand the human emotions. Observe activity, observe word inflection, observe the body language and facial expression, observe yourself and others making decisions and begin to identify the emotion(s) driving these various behaviors that you observe. And pay close attention to the speed at which the emotions operate, and the seeming autonomy and independence of their operation—oftentimes not in synchronization with thinking. When you truly learn and accept that there are only five primary emotions, the daily task of living becomes much easier as you will gain in self-knowledge and gain in the understanding of the behavior of others; and of additional importance, you will begin to know and understand how liberals function.

As you observe your elected officials on your TV and the news, YouTube presentations, or whatever and whomever, begin to pay close attention to what they say and how they say it. Observe their body language as well. Observe the degree and magnitude of emotional expression. Try your best to decipher which emotions(s) are driving their behavior. You will begin to know and perceive when those officials are lying or telling you the truth. Understand also that the backdrop and the templates of behavioral foundation of the current behavior of the individual is rooted in conditioning that may trace back to that individuals early formative years.

Consider it: God was absolutely brilliant (would we expect otherwise?) in coming up with our design. An infant or young child cries and sheds tears (both of which are expressions of the emotions of grief or fear in the infant or child) and these expressions serve as a signal to the parents (a mom and a dad) that something is amiss with the child. If the capacity to express (even unconsciously) these vital signs and signals didn't exist, then consequently, the very life and well-being of the child would be placed at great risk!

These emotional expressions of the child are unconscious and instinctive actions. An infant does not have the intellectual capacity or the ability of speech to tell the parents, "Hey guys, something is wrong. I'm going to shed a few tears right now so that you know!" In the child's early stages of development, the emotions automatically do that task for the child.

If that natural emotive process of the child is interrupted by parents, teachers, or caregivers (because those in authority carry within their own psyche negative attitudes or were themselves on the receiving end of negative beliefs or projections about the emotions which they then in turn readily internalized; and who themselves carry aberrant attitudes within their psyche regarding their own emotional expression) then the parent may ignore these present-day emotional expressions of the child, try to squash or repress them, or reprimand and scold the child for what they deem as aberrant behavior.

This begins to mold the template in the psyche of the child for the repression process. The natural instinctive emotive process in the child has been thwarted and negatively interrupted. This sets the stage for aberrant behavior patterns in that child which may carry well into the child's teen and adult life and remain there unaltered. And indeed, this young age is a vulnerable period. So much depends on the rhythmic functioning by those so influential in the formation of the child whether they are the parents, caregivers, or teachers, as they are all primary sources from which the young child learns. It is they from whom the child receives impressions from observing and imitating their behavior, and then internalizes and models that behavior, as very soon these various templates of behavior become indelibly owned by that child and become a part of their hard wiring. And once the hard wiring is in place, it becomes extremely difficult to alter or remove it.

Here we can perceive that this is yet another clue to the root causes of liberalism. Disruptions in the emotional development of the child may affect that person for a lifetime if there is not the proper alignment and a rhythmic foundation established for emotional function. And when emotional functions are subject to aberrant conditioning, one's ability to use logic and reason is negatively affected.

Allow this one reality and thought to thoroughly permeate every fragment of the gray matter of your brain. There is not **one** person on Earth who has not gone through this very important developmental period. Every person on Earth could possibly be subject to some degree of learning distortions during their progression from infancy through childhood. It is no surprise then that liberalism may affect so many. It is not a question of either/or, as the magnitude of the severity of the condition of liberalism lies on a continuum measured as a degree of magnitude of the disorder.

What does it matter of one's race, color, ethnicity, and religion? These characteristics do not matter, as they rank secondarily in importance in an examination of the traits that are held in common of each individual and all mankind. And one trait that remains consistent and steadfast to all people is having the same emotional component structure that may be subject to the risk of distortions of the personality as well as affecting behavioral manifestations, these outcomes of which are dependent in great part on the conditioning factors of the parents, teachers, and caregivers; in an environment encompassing the psychological, developmental, and behavioral. This emotional component of the personality structure, common to all humanity, is one of the very few things that the precept, "All Mankind are created equal," may be applied.

But now the notion of "All men are created equal" has been bastardized to include rights to do and have whatever, even to the extent to demand the right to control others; and to include an almost endless growing list of entitlements and demands, and added, without the individual having to put forth any work or effort to attain them.

Unfortunately, we're now beginning to observe in our nation, as the family unit is speedily disintegrating, the new collective caregiver. That is, state-run bureaucracies through the strong arm of the Department of Education or other massive government-run social institutions that are stepping in to take control of the indoctrination of our young children. And what's the result? It is poor academic outcomes, broken discipline, absenteeism and non-participation, and lack of motivation of our youth. Many of these same kids from broken families then run wild in the streets. No Hillary, in this case, it does not take a village! State- and government-run institutions, in an effort to ensure equality, are stretching the notion of equality to the limit, superimposing the notion of equality into areas where it does not belong. The liberal's notion of equality attempts to erase the fact of individual differences and in its place, create sameness. The notion of equality is extended to emotional expression as well, albeit, distorted as we'll see in the coming pages.

In the experience of the individual, if there should be a conflict between the natural instincts (included in this are the primary emotions), God-given natural law, and universal law versus distortions (with emphasis upon the word *distortions*) in religious indoctrination, social and educational liberal indoctrination, cultural influences, local ethnic customs, political correctness, the former of these two will invariably prevail according to cause and effect relationships, in the respect that either the adherence to and fulfillment of all the God-given laws, et cetera, will create a happy, fulfilled life and existence; or a dereliction and distortion of the same produced by artificial constructs and ephemeral relativistic morality will result in consequences that include humanity falling into disharmony and into un-rhythmic existence. Non-conformance to God-given and universal natural law will invariably create adverse consequences for all humanity.

Top-down government control aimed at the homogenization of individuals, along with the sudden evolution and change imposed upon humanity and erasing long-standing, time-tested social institutions and moral standards, and an assault on the family structure—does not work. Under such state-run bureaucracies, the risk is ever-present that statistics of the mass of youngsters becomes more important than the beauty of the uniqueness of the individual—hence, the lesson to be learned is that individuals cannot be perceived nor dealt with as statistical units nor dealt with as belonging to a class. It seems nowadays all are being split into classes, which is leading to the unintended consequence of the severe Balkanization of America.

A good example is the middle class. Does anyone really know how to define the middle class? Obama, the Democrats, and Republicans talk a lot about the middle class. But the middle class as traditionally perceived has been changing if not disappearing; however, that does not stop them from referring to the middle class as if the middle class is an enduring quantity that must be protected.

Yes indeed, the emotions are the primary drivers of human behavior and they will continue to serve in that capacity, spanning the time from the early acquired predispositions of behavior from the period of infancy and childhood, and throughout the entire life of the individual!

A warm smile on the face of the infant or child, expressing the primary emotion of love, displayed towards the parents (a mom and a dad) conveys comfort and contentment. At that stage of development, a child does not stop to engage his or her thinking, and therefore reason or think to him or herself, "OK, now I'm content and feel just great; think I'll smile!" It's all instinctual on the part of that still unconscious child, and those emotional reactions happen spontaneously, quickly, and automatically. It also serves as a wordless communication to the parents, "All is well with me."

In the same way that the child unconsciously displays the emotion of love to mom and dad by that warm smile, it is during this period of development that the child's foundation in self-love and self-respect begins to form. On a primitive, timeless unconscious level, the child knows that love is (or should be) forthcoming from the parents and the child perceives, "I am loved; therefore, I am worthy of love and respect."

If—and this is the big if—that child has the proper rudiments in place to create a steadfast foundation in self-love and self respect—the positive attitude so created from such a foundation would in the lifetime of that individual be projected outward and extend to each and every person they will meet and interact with in life, extending to all those individuals they encounter, with the very same love and respect that they have for themselves.

Therefore, they would never have the need to lash out at their fellow man because they would be free of having been inculcated with learned hatred based upon bastardized and distorted religious indoctrination of whatever variety of religion, distorted social and educational ideology, top-down governmental authoritarian political ideology, and all the other garden variety yet noxious distortions acquired in their personality learned from parents, teachers, caregivers, core curriculum, and from state- and government-run bureaucratic institutions.

I am fascinated by watching the film clips of cultural explorers as they go deep into jungle terrain and discover a long-lost and forgotten ancient primitive tribe of people—living in the same traditions as unchanged today as they existed for hundreds if not thousands of years. The various tribes of the American Indians, as found at the time the first Europeans set foot on the Americas, are representative of such cultures. For as much as could be determined, those ancient cultures remained relatively unchanged for hundreds if not thousands of years.

What is most striking is watching the film clips of current-day cultures of the very young children compiled by the explorers. The children are smiling and laughing, though having nothing more materially than scant clothing, makeshift shelters, food, and for toys and entertainment, they play in the dirt with sticks and stones. They display total contentment.

The reason for their apparent total contentment, I will surmise, is because they live in emotional rhythm and harmony; free of any adverse influences stemming from emotional dysfunction in the family unit, free of all the influences that come from modernism and all the negative aspects generated from such; whether from education, technology, the proliferation of material goods, et cetera. If nothing more, this simple illustration should prove that happiness comes from within and is not dependent upon conditions arising outside of one's existence as liberals would have us all believe.

But then, some may put forth the silly argument and suggest, "So are you saying we should revert back to living a rather primitive agrarian lifestyle in mud and straw huts and take up the practice, as Sheryl Crow suggests, and crap in the woods and use one sheet of toilet paper?"[1] Well, maybe she didn't say crap in the woods, but she did advocate one sheet of toilet paper. No, ladies and gentlemen, of course not! That's not at all what I'm advocating as if we should revert back to practices of the Stone Age.

The many decades of the progression into modernism, with all our material goods and wealth and all that it entails, has added to the challenge that each individual finds him or herself in. Desiring and obtaining material wealth is not inherently antithetical to one's quest for a spiritual foundation. One may be the wealthiest person on earth, with every material comfort imaginable and still be very much attuned to their own spiritual quest and destiny!

It's a matter of personal choice where one wants to direct their energy. We simply work and carry on in the current environment we find ourselves in with all the added and increased challenges, which is not to say that an unbridled quest for material wealth may override one's spiritual quest. It's a matter of each individual choosing their priorities. As will be stated in this book more than once, the greater the challenge, the greater the reward. Without challenge and choice, there is no spiritual evolution. In my opinion, modernism presents a much greater challenge for one to pursue a spiritual quest in the ordinary conditions of life we find ourselves in today.

But the liberals would have us believe that the civil and social unrest, and the terrorism displayed by Muslims in Islamic countries as they take up a life of hate, terror, and murder, is caused by lack of jobs, opportunity, or material goods, and of course, they place blame for this lack on the United States of America.

This argument is also used to explain the crime, poverty, murder, and degradation experienced in the predominantly black urban communities and other economically depressed areas of our country; that is, a lack of jobs, quality education, and material goods. It is the same vacuous excuse furthered by President Barack Hussein Obama, Al Sharpton, our liberal senators and congressmen, the ACLU, and others, that the rioting in Ferguson, Missouri, or Baltimore, Maryland, was caused by the lack of jobs and material needs (not to mention their additional excuse, due to civil rights violations or discrimination).

This view is totally wrong-headed, as it supports the view that the causes of one's destructive behavior always lie outside of one, and therefore outside of one's control. How can a primitive society, as pointed out earlier, certainly living in much more extreme conditions of lack than those in Ferguson or Baltimore, live in such harmony? If the logic of these liberals was accurate, these primitive societies should have self-destructed centuries ago and destroyed anyone or anything in near proximity to them! Then, all traces of them would have long ago been destroyed, and the irony is, we would not even be aware that they existed at all and certainly not be talking about them in this very moment!

But the forces and conditions which serve to forever alter and destroy these ancient cultures are the relentless progression of technology and modernization. That is what is accountable for their destruction and disappearance over the last few centuries. For countless generations, these primitive cultures were maintained by long-established social mores, tribal laws, and customs that they steadfastly adhered to and enforced. They were truly the first to exemplify the practice that the best politics begins at the local level. For them, politics began at the local level and there it was steadfastly and easily maintained at the smaller groupings of tribal level, as then all in the community were aware and involved participants.

This stands in sharp contrast to the bigness of governments, institutions, and bureaucracies of our modern era, in which dramatic changes can be superimposed upon a nation-state in the space of a few short years. For the fact is that as the numbers of the masses grow and proliferate, a disconnect begins to happen between leadership and the people. The individual citizen, who should be by all means fully alert and vigilant to the many factors exerting control over him, becomes lost and immersed in the sheer mass of numbers, and is instead overwhelmed, immersed, and anesthetized into a sleep-state of non-participation. Then, the leadership, gathering enough power and will over the people, may initiate changes in the culture in short spaces of time in accordance with the aberrant and demagogic beliefs of the leadership and those in power. Seemingly, the individual becomes powerless to act.

One need only look at recent events at how so many succumbed to and submitted their will to, "Change you can believe in." No one knew what it meant, but they believed in a slogan and blindly followed it! Edmund Burke, in his writings of the eighteenth century, said,

But one of the first and most leading principles on which the commonwealth and the laws are consecrated, is lest the temporary possessors and life-renters in it, unmindful of what they have received from their ancestors, or of what is due to their posterity, should act as if they were the entire masters; that they should not think it amongst their rights to cut off the entail, or commit waste on the inheritance, by destroying at their pleasure the whole original fabric of their society; hazarding to leave to those who come after them, a ruin instead of an habitation—and teaching these successors as little to respect their contrivances, as they had themselves respected the institutions of their forefathers. By this unprincipled facility of changing the state as often,

and as much, and in as many ways as there are
floating fancies or fashions, the whole chain and
continuity of the commonwealth would be broken.
No one generation could link with the other.
Men would become little better than the flies of
summer."[2]

Now, after eight years of the liberal Obama administration, are all of you happy with this change you can believe in? Do you know what this change means and whether or not it is complete? How can you when you don't know what it meant to begin with?

These ancient primitive cultures were not subject to these changes. They managed to remain unchanged for thousands of years free of the influence of any forces from without, but of greater importance, free of any forces from within that would derail their society. They lived a rhythmic existence.

The only reliable antidote against these fancies, fashions, and utopian dreams that any nation-state may practice is a steadfast adherence to universal God-given laws of conduct and behavior, and in the case of the United States, additionally, strict adherence to our founding documents, which themselves were derived from and constructed upon God's Law, the laws of nature, unalienable laws, natural law, et cetera.

The dysfunction in these severely impacted black or white communities is caused by lack of and/or distorted parental authority, or subversive indoctrination in education and other intrusive government intervention. The actions of the rioters (and those supporting them) in both Ferguson and Baltimore were driven by deeply repressed hatred and fear.

The Great Society, instituted by Lyndon Johnson in the 1960s to freely supply food, education, and housing to impoverished areas, has proved to be an abysmal failure for the greater reason that the individual was robbed of individual initiative and then willingly submitted their will and fate to the state, and in truth, ushered in a new form of slavery—that is, slavery to the state and to all the many false promises. Do you think it's possible that many of the slaves living in the pre-emancipation era were more joyful and content than many of the black population today living under this new form of slavery? How would you compare the two? It's a rhetorical question. What do you think?

CHAPTER 6

INDIVIDUAL DYNAMICS OF THE PRIMARY HUMAN EMOTIONS

I f one were to randomly select from a large bed of pebbles all of those that appeared were of the same size, one could make conclusions about all of those selected regarding the general size and shape, the various hues and colors of the pebbles, and about the average weight of each. But if one were to isolate only one pebble and expect that it would precisely fit and match into any of the general parameters concluded about all the pebbles—it would not. One would soon realize that any one pebble is different from any other. No two are exactly alike.

And so it is with human beings. There is a sharp contrast when comparing and discussing the dynamics of people of the collective and large groups with that of the early unfolding and unconscious progression of things happening on the level of emotional unfolding and the development of thinking in the individual.

Thinking does not begin to develop in an accelerated fashion, certainly not to the extent of even rudimentary multi-layered concepts; logic, and reason, until the age of seven—give or take a year or two. Each develops at a different pace. And no, Hillary, the brain is not 80 percent developed by age three as you tried to convince the Americans listening to one of your recent speech declaring your bid to run for presidency in the 2016 election.

But I will ask you, dear reader, if you recall intellectual memories from the age of zero to one; or from the age of one to two; or from two to three, and so on? Most do not remember much of anything of an intellectual nature until getting into the age of three, four, and then more numerous and pronounced memories from five, six, and so on.

It is true that one may possess long-past images and still pictures of their life imprinted on their memory, but it is more rare or unlikely that memories of an experience of logic, along with all the connected components of that experience, are carried forward, although those moments of the experience of logic (call it a *eureka moment*) carried with it a certain taste of wakefulness. Do you have memories of such a moment? This goes directly to the heart of the issue of brain development and as we'll see, emotional development as well.

A child may have a memory of when he/she learned that two plus two equals four, but does that child remember the exact time and place that he/she had the momentary epiphany of learning and logic? Do you? To arrive at a position of logic requires a consolidation of two or more divergent factors. If one is prevailed upon by their emotions that in some manner may be distorted or repressed and which serve to intrude upon and preempt thinking, reason, or logic, it is far less likely that moments of reason or logic may be regularly achieved as reason and logic is not a byproduct of emotion, and may be inhibited and thwarted by distorted emotion.

Enhanced and subsequently remembered memories of a very early age are due primarily to the influence of the emotional quadrant. But, distortions in the proper unfolding of emotional development may inhibit and hinder the intellectual learning of the individual, either in terms of hindrances in learning by the laws of association, and certainly inhibitions in the development of logic. I would go so far as to say that the inhibition of proper emotional development may also inhibit an individual's physical development. Consider the fact that a child laden with all sorts of fears may be subject to overactive adrenal production which can have detrimental physical effects.

Most early intellectual learning happens in accordance with the laws of association. Many of us may be familiar with very young children who show immense capacity to learn facts and information, but this learning has nothing to do necessarily with learning the dynamics of reason or logic. Text books designed to teach kindergarten and first graders to learn rudimentary counting by equating, for example, the numeral four with pictures of four apples is an example of learning by association.

But, some individuals may find that pronounced emotional traumas experienced during those early years become indelibly imprinted upon their memory. Those memories that involved intense emotions of fear, grief, or anger (anger particularly displayed by others and directed at the young individual) or emotional experiences that are of such traumatic impact that the conscious memory of them, also may re-introduce those painful experiences. Therefore, these memories may be repressed into forgetfulness by the individual. But the repressed energy can't remain static indefinitely and sooner or later the emotion associated with it will break forth. That energy may manifest in some manner, for example, as various phobias during the life of the individual or as depressive episodes. Perhaps even as rageful periodic outbursts.

Another key attribute and characteristic of the emotions is that they operate with a different energy than that of the brain and thinking function operates. The emotions operate with a much finer and more volatile, quicker-acting energy, that may be identified as a form and gradation of psychic energy, in contrast to the energy of the thinking (brain) quadrant, which operates with a slower-acting energy more along the order of electrical energy. But yet, this energy utilized by the brain is of a much finer gradation that that of which the physical body and all its musculature and various organs use to carry out its operation.

That's right, you may think of electrical energy as operating at a great rate of speed, and that's basically correct relative to your physical existence, but psychic energy is so much more volatile and quick acting! It's like identifying the energy used by the emotions using the analogy of comparing it with high octane racing fuel; while the function of thinking uses fuel or energy analogous to diesel fuel, a lower-grade, slower-acting form of energy.

And to continue the metaphor, the energy used by the physical body is along the lines of low-grade heating oil—it is slow-burning and slow-acting. Think of it this way: just as raw petroleum is broken down as it makes its way through the refining process into the various by-products; that is, fine, medium, and coarser elements, so too food ingested into the human body is broken down and refined into various gradations of energy for use by the human species—all into a form that can be utilized by the emotions, brain, or physical body.

It is only natural that many of us automatically take it for granted that we need food to stay alive. But does it occur to our thinking process that we comprehend that the physical body, the brain, and the emotions each use a different gradation of energy? The human body is, in effect, a miniature refinery. Where do you think the energy comes from to operate the body, brain, and emotions? Those of you who are familiar with the concept of psychic energy; well, the emotions use and emit this kind of energy.

To continue an extension of the metaphor, the fuel of the physical body is of the order of low-grade heating oil or even wood kindling, a much coarser fuel. Those of you who believe in and support fuel economy as it pertains to your automobile, do you also support fuel usage and economy as it pertains to your human body? The emotional component uses a more finely refined and valuable energy produced by the body. Distortions, repressions, and aberrations in the individual emotional component automatically force the body to direct more energy to the emotional component. This results in very poor fuel economy for the individual, in regard both to bodily and especially emotional functioning, and depletes the body of valuable necessary energy that should otherwise serve toward the greater well-being of the individual. This is why those with emotional dysfunctions tend to be lethargic and negative due to them living in a perpetual state of depletion of energy.

And the most damaging effect produced is what I call *emotional pollution*. The liberals are responsible for the great volumes of emotional pollution discharged into the environment. This pollution will manifest in the form of distorted lies and twisted beliefs, a great deal of nonsense in the media, distortions and manipulations via all sorts of polls, distortions and lies that proceed from our governing elitists, those hate-filled encounters and interactions among the populace, fanatic adherence to political correctness, and the expelling of a great deal of hot air in the form of CO_2. Thankfully, CO_2 is not a pollutant, a belief that many of the liberal idiots cling to and would like all to believe. But in the least, the hot air and CO_2 expelled is helping our trees. Those liberals, including President Barack Hussein Obama, so concerned about conserving energy should look into this.

How many of you have said that a certain physical activity has completely drained you of energy? Or, after an intense period of directing your thought and attention to a project—you are mentally drained?

Otherwise, who of you have stated on occasion that you are emotionally drained? Periodically I have heard it said by someone that when in the presence of a certain individual, "They zap me of emotional energy." It is impossible for someone to zap you of energy as if they have the power to do that to you. Rather, it has to do with what's going on within you and your own emotional structure. It is up to you to examine that. Dare we by further extension speculate that by further refinement of energy in the physical body, our spiritual self may be nourished and fed? After all, we do possess a spiritual quadrant. Generally, due to wastage, poor economy, aberrant behavior, and general negativity, there is little if any food value left available to feed the spiritual quadrant. Yes, I know, the naysayers may all come out of the woodwork to doubt this. But for those who accept that each individual is endowed with a soul, a spark of the Divine, do you think it's just placed in your body at birth and then you have no responsibility to care, nourish, and nurture it so that it grows and expands? Those of you who are planting a garden, do you expect you can stick a seed in the ground, then come back in six weeks to harvest mature fruit from the plant without having to put forth any nurturing and care?

Indeed, psychic energy and emotional energy is a much more volatile and quicker acting energy. That's why so-called *knee-jerk* reactions exhibited by some are based primarily upon emotional reactions. How many of you have looked back upon an experience and said, "I should have thought before I acted?" Your action was overridden and driven by emotion. The more volatile, quick-acting energy of emotion superseded that of thinking. How many of you have gone out to buy an expensive car, only to realize the next day that you made a very stupid decision. That's because you were under the spell of your emotions (they call it *under the ether* at the auto dealerships). You may be forced to admit to yourself that after the deed (and deal) is done that your thinking, reason, and logic were not properly engaged. How many of you have gone into an important meeting without having your emotions in check, and rather than engage your thinking, you emotionally overreacted and wound up holding the short end of the stick in the deal, if not made to look stupid? How many of you have fallen into a relationship driven by the emotion of love, and only some time later awaken to the true reality of what you really did; that is… that you made a good decision. Okay, be honest, how many of you thought I was going to say otherwise?

Many of you may have witnessed or experienced firsthand at a sports event, just prior to the opening bell or whistle or when all things are going well for the winning team, the announcer may say, "Can't you feel the excitement and electricity in the air filling the entire stadium?" The fact is, this is not energy of the order of electricity; rather, it is psychic energy produced by the emotions, and this kind of energy may be projected outside of one and indeed it may be perceived and picked up by those around in close proximity.

Speaking of sports events, if one desires to witness prime examples of the working and display of the five primary emotions, a sports event such as a football game provides an excellent opportunity for study, as this event presents a great working laboratory for observing all the primary emotions at work. Another noteworthy yearly event is "The Road to the Final Four" basketball tournament. Observe the crowds and observe how the individual emotions are displayed. Observe yourself and how you may be drawn into the action via your own emotional experience and how your own emotions engage on different levels.

The following are just a few typical examples observable at a sports event to draw from to identify how each one of the emotions manifest, but the next time you're at a sports event, observe for yourself how the primary emotions manifest and that includes yourself.

First, the donning of sports apparel or waving of banners represents the unifying identification of the many individuals present as they congregate together at the event—demonstrative of the love they have for the team. This experience of love could be directed to particular players, the coaches, the sponsoring city, or whatever.

Next, the intense desire and excitement multiplies within the many individuals present, both on the part of the players and the fans as they envision their team winning the game or the championship, and then relishing in the enjoyment of that achievement. This overall experience is identified in the emotion of jealousy and zeal.

Intense anger may be generated often and within many individuals at that sports event—by that late hit on your favorite quarterback, by a poorly executed play by your favorite team, if someone purposefully deflates footballs to aid in gaining a winning edge over the opponent, or if it is perceived that the referee made a very bad call to the detriment of your team. Then, the anger and the name-calling will likely follow.

The emotion of fear is acutely experienced by the wide receiver when he has to go high on that mid route to catch an errant pass, knowing that he will take a huge hit from the defenders!

The emotion of grief is fully experienced when the game-winning field-goal kick attempt goes awry, resulting in your favorite team losing the game.

And these are just some representations of the five primary emotions that may be observable drawing from the example of the sports event, but I'm sure you can associate many more examples of linking a primary emotion with any number of circumstances at such a sports event. These primary emotions may be experienced numerous times and in concert with other emotions, as these examples of the sports event demonstrate.[2]

---

[2] *While touching on the subject of football, it is this very sport, especially at the professional level, that the liberals are attacking with a vengeance. They believe it is far too dangerous a sport and now even Congress is sticking their noses into the discussion. One issue dominating the media and one of which Congress (and even the president) are sticking their nose into, has to do with head injuries. So what does our leadership do? They want to legislate, pass more laws and regulations. Hey, Congressman and Mr. President, it's an occupational hazard. Many occupations have a certain degree of occupational hazard or risk associated with them. The organization will figure out a way to*

Of interest to observe at a given sports event is that in every specific instance in which the facts of the circumstance are ample to illicit an emotional response; each individual's emotional reaction to the same event may be slightly different. One person may react to the circumstance in a reserved fashion and another may react vehemently. Humans, by their nature and due to their intellectual learning, may influence, repress, alter, or enhance emotional learning and conditioning to the extent that emotional reactions appear individualized with some differences even though all witnessed the very same event. Generally, these differences in emotional responses are contingent almost totally on the early conditioning factors to which the individual was subject.

---

take care of and regulate itself. If these elected officials, these servants of we the people, were really concerned about head injuries, they would direct more attention to the real head injuries taking place in foreign lands; that is, the head injuries suffered by Christians and others at the hands of extremist Muslims; that is, beheadings!

On the surface, though, it appears their concern is about the safety issue, or they have an issue with the team's choice of a mascot, eg, the Redskins. I believe the real issue is the fact that the liberals are thwarted in their effort to intrude with their affirmative action agenda, and additionally, it's all about controlling your life. To earn a job and a top spot on any team has everything to do with talent, ability, and hard work. One's culture, skin color, ethnicity, religious persuasion, or sexual orientation has nothing to do with landing a spot on the team. Each player earns his spot on that football team first and foremost by hard work and sheer ability. This is what frustrates the liberal, because up to now, these things are totally out of their ability to control.

If one desires to witness emotional reactions free of any repressions, inhibitions, intellectual manipulations, et cetera, one need only to observe mammals. Mammals posses the very same five primary emotions as humans; and furthermore, mammals are also much more adept at expressing the emotions in a natural manner as they have no learned screening process to repress or alter spontaneous emotional expression.

Elephants make a great test case for observation. Elephants may spend days experiencing the grief over the loss of one of their herd. We've all heard the term, *survival of the fittest*. Generally, this term is used in reference to the mammalian kingdom, for indeed, to survive, the mammal must exist in its peak ability of physical and emotional prowess, otherwise, if not, it will die. Should there be any less concern for the human? No! The human species must also function at his peak of physical, emotional, and intellectual prowess in order to survive. But the truth is, many of the human species have a severely distorted emotional pathology subjecting them to risks that will take them down and they will lose in their fight for survival. And worse yet, disharmonies in human emotional functioning will prevent one from fully opening to their spiritual facet.

Mammals are much more adept at 'picking up' and sensing the energy of the emotions projected by humans. Mammals are adept at perceiving instantly what a human is feeling and will respond accordingly. A primary emotion often projected by humans in the presence of mammals is fear. Many people fear domestic dogs, and a dog will immediately perceive if a human is experiencing (projecting) fear. Domestic dogs and especially wild animals, when perceiving fear in an individual, will interpret it as enmity or aggression, and may possibly attack the person because the animal perceives the fear projected by the human as a threat!

Humans, due to their mammalian instinctual heritage, also have the innate capacity to pick up and perceive emotions from other people at an unconscious level, but generally not to the same keen degree as mammals, because the human intellectualizing process gets in the way of fully instinctively perceiving the emotions—especially the further into adulthood the person grows. That's why young children pick up and automatically perceive, though at an unconscious level, the emotional energy projected by adults in their presence and begin to internalize and model the emotions of the parents (a mom and a dad), and in a manner, the hard wiring begins to become established and set in place, and the child automatically becomes just like them. Many of you may remember the song in the seventies, "Cats in the Cradle", by Harry Chapin, a ballad about a father and son, and the conditioning factors surrounding that relationship.[1] The son became a product of his environment and grew up to be 'just like him'.

The intellect of the child is not yet developed to impede or repress the emotions; the unconscious instinctive perception and the display of the emotions as they were inculcated then takes dominance in their behavior. Many of you may have observed how sometimes young children exhibit a spontaneous intense dislike for someone, or contrariwise, may instantly like someone. This happens because young children are still much more attuned to their unconscious promptings via the emotions, and therefore, are more directly guided by the influence of the emotions. It is with the aging of the child that the intellect forms and grows in which case the attunement to the emotions at a conscious level begins to abate having been overridden by the thinking function, by the inculcation of various overriding beliefs, and by various repression processes.

If an individual has succeeded in bringing their emotions into rhythm and harmony, especially the emotion of fear, when in the presence of a flesh-eating mammal, the mammal may not necessarily attack the person. But in the instance of the mammal sensing fear in the individual, it may be motivated and stimulated to attack the person out of a perception and interpretation of enmity. But I will not encourage anyone to test this theory by stepping into the cage of a large lion if you happen to believe you have your emotions in rhythm. The lion may still attack you for the simple reason that it is hungry! And due to human emotional dysfunctions, I understand that flesh-eating mammals have developed a particularly keen taste for liberals! And just because you think you identify with conservatism, don't be so sure of yourself; you may be a CINO, so do not cast caution to the wind.[3]

---

[3] *Do not, however, expect that the same sort of encounter will produce the same scenario with reptiles. They, being cold-blooded and without the same range of emotions as warm-blooded creatures and certainly humans, if hungry, will attack and eat you regardless of your inner*

The overall behavior of the child begins to be governed by the emotions at that early age. The entire psychological, developmental, and environmental climate in which the child is immersed begins to permeate and superimpose itself onto the child, albeit at a very unconscious level and mode.

The most dominant and influential figures in the life of the child are, of course, the parents. It is from the parents that the child, as early as one year of age, will take on the very same psychic and behavioral characteristics of the parents, a great deal of which is unconsciously learned by imitating and modeling behavior of the parents.

If the child is born into a household with liberal parents, the chances are good that the child will grow up to be a liberal. Contrary-wise, if the parents are of a conservative persuasion, the odds are more likely weighted towards the child growing up to be conservative. But these are just broad generalizations and nothing is guaranteed nor assured. There are far too many incalculable variables at play. A child reared in a conservative household could be changed into a liberal if subjected to the constant brain-washing of liberal teachers—kindergarten through the upper

---

psychological composition. They do not possess the same range of emotions as mammals or humans and do not give a damn about you to the extent of caring to size you up emotionally. They may see you as both a threat and a meal! How do you think the term cold-blooded came to be associated with dastardly, murderous human behavior? Cold-blooded behaviors of an individual result when that person is cut off from or are in denial of their emotions. Can you identify anyone like that?

educational levels. And vice versa, a child from a liberal household may through a stroke of fortuitous grace, be subject to conditions that will mold the child into a worthy conservative. Many of you are familiar with Juan Williams, the extremely liberal news commentator on FOX. It so happens that his son, Raffi, is very conservative.[2] So there you have it. As this example shows, nothing is certain, and any notion of equality of experience in this realm does not exist!

It is during the very early childhood stages of development—roughly the period encompassing the age progression of year one through seven—during which the repression process of the emotions begins to become fixed and firmly rooted. When the emotions begin to be regularly and repetitively repressed, it is inevitable that at some time in the future the intrusion of this dammed-up repressed energy will assert itself into the domain of feeling and into the cognitive/thinking quadrant of the person resulting in the disharmonic functioning of one's thinking and reasoning.

This process, occurring regularly and often repetitively in the early years of the child, will be referred to as the implantation and firm fixation of one's *basic attitudes*, due to the repetitive patterning effect of factors that are classified as developmental, environmental, and psychological. This period of development during the childhood years of one through seven occurs prior to the formation of the intellect. If this intellectual development took place in a way other than the way it does, let's say, if it were fully developed by age seven, it would be a different story. Then, a developed intellect would serve in the capacity of a monitoring or censoring device which would influence and affect emotional learning; but without that degree of intellectual censoring, a child's learning in the emotional domain becomes steadfastly entrenched, though in many ways in an unconscious manner, and henceforth will manifest from unconscious motivations. The *basic attitudes* form the foundational templates of behavior of the person from which most if not all of their orientation to their life experience, their interactions, motivations, and participation in all their day to day life activities commence! And what is the foundation of the *basic attitudes?*—the emotions, of course! And upon what are the behaviors and attitudes of the modern-day liberal based?—aberrations in emotional development, of course!

This sets the stage and establishes the template—as the child grows into the teen years and then into adulthood, these templates of behavior become even more fixated both consciously and unconsciously in the psyche of the individual. *Basic attitudes* may manifest in a variety of ways as for instance forming the foundation of certain beliefs. Due to the fact that the foundation of the basic attitudes is unconscious to the person, the behavioral characteristic of 'inflexibility' may manifest in all the various life activities of that person. Try having a rational argument with someone who is firmly entrenched in a certain (emotional) belief. In these instances, belief preempts real knowledge of facts and objective knowledge. This barrier of inflexibility of the person may not be broken through, even though subjected to generous amounts of sound reason or logic. Truly, a decidedly liberal characteristic: The more one attempts to break through this barrier—the more defensiveness one will encounter from that individual accompanied by reactionary behavior of anger and fear which will be readily displayed from the person even to the point of them lashing out at you or attacking you.

These *basic attitudes* may become rooted in an individual and consequently manifest in such a way that the person will be perceived as having an *'attitude'*. This is where the expression comes from, that is, having an *'attitude'*. Of course, you've heard that expression— someone is said to have an attitude—generally perceived in a negative sense as when one is accused of having a *'bad attitude'*. And depending on which emotion forms the foundation and the configuration of the basic attitude—most commonly, the basis of an attitude is driven by repressed anger and fear. You will always know when you meet up with one of these individuals. Their behavior may manifest as perpetually negative, with an underlying current of anger. Perhaps they are often in a complaining mode of how bad and unfair life is, and everyone is out to get them and take advantage of them. Doesn't this behavior remind you of liberal behavior? They will often accuse the rich of taking advantage of them even to the extent that the total gain of the rich was acquired by treading on the backs of the poor and downtrodden.

And ironically it is often those who are very rich who join the side of those who are on the attack! Ted Kennedy was a fine example of such a person. Other examples are Nancy Pelosi, Barbara Boxer, and Harry Reid—just to name a few, and the list compiled from those in Washington, DC, is quite long. It seems these many liberals are always taking up the crusade for the 'poor'. But don't be fooled by these liberals. They were only patronizing the poor to get their vote. Do you really believe that they actually really care about the poor?

The behavior of those with a bad attitude may be characterized by undue aggression or defensiveness, often seeking someone or something to blame. Those chronically affected with a negative attitude or a bad attitude may have a permanent scowl fixated upon their face. And by the way, bad attitudes may be found in those of the socio-economic class of both the rich and poor. Bad attitudes are an equal-opportunity intruder. If you broach certain topics with them, it is as if not a sliver of the light of reason may enter into this dark cavernous enclave of one of their frozen attitudes. And if you press the topic, they will become even angrier with you and may cut off the discussion abruptly. It is as if in the past, they were given a post-hypnotic suggestion that when such-and-such happens, they will be unable to move off their position as if frozen in mind and attitude.

It is this hard wiring of sorts which will accompany the individual throughout life, and cannot be altered or removed except without a great deal of introspection, effort, pain, and sacrifice. And in regard to sacrifice, one may ask, "Sacrifice what? What are you talking about?" Well, it may mean sacrificing a perception one has of him or herself, sacrificing a trait which in the grand scheme of things does not serve the person well (which the liberal will never come to realize nor do they want to because the removal of it will take away their justification for their beliefs and behavior, and will be as if their foundation is ripped from under them). It may mean opening one's eyes to what has been hiding in plain sight.

When faced with giving up a false notion of oneself, a person may become very angry, fearful, and defensive. Having to give up something may stimulate fear within a person. It will be as if the person's entire psychological foundation upon which all their beliefs, attitudes, motivations, et cetera, are based, is now shaken to the core and they are facing an annihilation of the picture of who they think they are, and all their perceptions of themselves are at risk of nullification! It is a difficult step for one to separate and quell the identifications to which they are firmly attached, with all their false notions of what they believe and who they believe they think they are.

The sort of sacrifice just discussed, is more of a 'psychological' sacrifice, not to be confused with a material sacrifice which is more associated with goal achievement, that is, if you want to graduate summa cum laude from Harvard, you don't spend hours of the day texting your friends or watching junk TV. Instead you hit the books! Oftentimes, if you want to achieve something, you must set aside all things that will block or slow down your progression to your desired goal.

As a listener and observer of radio talk shows and TV, I've listened to numerous people call in to talk shows—and the caller refuses to answer direct questions and make simple acknowledgements about an issue. This is due to fear; fear of change and fear of admitting that for very long they have existed under misperceptions which they fear may need to be given up. That is what I'm referring to in regard to the notion of sacrifice. Before the implantation of something new and beneficial, the old must be removed, discarded, and sacrificed. A part of them that does not serve them well needs to be removed. And that job can only be initiated by them alone. That job can only become effective when the individual opens their eyes and sees the need of it.

When we say, *basic attitudes*, remember, it is in the plural that we speak of them. *Basic attitudes* may exist in opposition and difference to other *basic attitudes*. In extreme cases, this sort of behavior manifests as multiple personality disorder, as you may know is when a split occurs in the persons psyche and different personalities will manifest (generally unknown to one another via the persons conscious thought and awareness). But for the moment, we're not necessarily talking about extreme cases such as was represented in the film production of a case of split personality in *Three Faces of Eve*. No, lesser instances abound in which those in leadership and authority will made a declaration one day (from one part of their consciousness), and (another part of them) will say the exact opposite the next day, and all the while they may be fully cognizant of what they are doing and saying; as for example when President Barack Hussein Obama says, "If you like your health care plan, you may keep your health care plan," knowing all the while that it was a bold-faced lie.

Such an individual creates buffer zones or blinders in their mind and refuses to acknowledge and see outside those buffer zones. Hence, they cultivate and learn to exhibit inflexibility in their beliefs though contrary beliefs may exist simultaneously within them. And furthermore, don't you think that those types of individuals, in carrying out this sort of behavior, surely must look upon you, the citizen, with the utmost of disdain and contempt as if you must be a complete ignoramus?

Everyone, no doubt, has had encounters with someone in regard to a certain issue. Let's say that with this certain person you are in total disagreement about topic XYZ. And let's give you the benefit that in this most objective of all worlds in which the discussion is taking place, you are absolutely correct in your position! Then, no matter how many facts, data, and information you present to this argumentative someone, they cannot be swayed off their position! And the more facts, information, reason, and logic you submit to them— the angrier and more aggressively they dig their heels in, resolutely refusing to open their mind. They will equivocate, try to switch the argument, or lie—anything to avoid looking into the mirror of themselves. And you can bet that supporting this impassive foundation is a deeply entrenched *basic attitude(s)*.

This, ladies and gentlemen, should supply another symptom of the roots of 'liberalism'. The person sticks to their point of view not from a position of logic and reason, but from a purely emotional foundation, albeit, still unconscious to them. Generally, the main driving emotion is fear. And the word that best describes these immovable positions is irrational! Furthermore, it is a basic attitude that bolsters this foundation.

We all know what fanaticism is. It is closely linked and akin to irrationality. What we've just been describing is also the basis of fanaticism. Fanaticism is not an emotion, but rather an activity and actions stemming from narrow indelible beliefs, although fanaticism is driven by intense emotion of either a repressed or open nature. Fanaticism is generally a distortion and imbalance of the primary emotions regardless of the brand of fanaticism engaged in or the object to which the fanatical behavior is directed. Surely, religious fanaticism must be the absolute worst kind of fanaticism as those so inclined justify their horrific actions as if God (or Allah or whoever) himself endorses and supports such heinous actions, such as what we witness taking place by radical Muslim terrorists! Surely this is an example of the ultimate bastardization of the Islamic (or any) religion!

Regarding those so frozen into their point of view, if their position was suddenly made fully conscious to them (and at the risk of them being driven to insanity), they would see the error of their logic and reason (or lack of), and come over to your point of view by virtue of pure reason. But the primary emotions forcing their positions are generally fear, anger, and add to that a state of being called *guilt*. And here, we are not referring to guilt to be associated with the experience of the transgression of a universal God-given law, which would trigger what is commonly termed *remorse*—the foundation of which is the human conscience (which in turn is grounded in our spiritual facet). No, we are referring to guilt experienced from a transgression of this ubiquitous relativistic morality, otherwise known as political correctness, which has become very pervasive and insidious in our country and culture. The purpose of political correctness (and its use as a tool) is to create fear and to manipulate and control the masses. And those who sponsor, initiate, and support this ubiquitous political correctness, also do so out of a framework of their own internal fear. You must always be mindful of what was said earlier about the emotions. The emotions are the drivers of behavior and fear absolutely is a primary driver of behavior. In the hands of despots, dictators, and ideologues, the use of creating and instilling fear becomes a tool to manipulate and control. Do you at any time wonder how despots and dictators may harbor their own internal fear despite them possessing so much power? Hitler, Stalin, Kim Jong Un, and most other dictators and despots were (and are) extremely fearful and paranoid. Lurking around every corner was someone plotting to undermine or kill them.

We need look no further than Washington, DC, to witness milder examples of those fearful of losing their position and power. It is safe to speculate and sad to say that most of our elected officials in Washington, DC, are among these fearful individuals. President Barack Hussein Obama is much too fearful to appear on FOX News, and FOX News is not even a wholly conservative news purveyor, as if Obama should be fearful of it. And to put this in perspective, we'll get into much deeper discussions of fear in a coming chapter. For now, understand that we are born into the world with only two natural fears—the fear of falling and the fear of loud noises. We have been talking about artificially created fears.

Have you noticed that this political correctness is actually loathed by so very many, but then it seems to continually spread and grow? Do you often discover that fact in conversation? Then who or what sustains it? And why are so many fearful of transgressing it? It is because if you transgress it, guilt will be heaped upon you! But then you yourself allow this guilt to be internalized within yourself. Why? Why do you behave so cowardly and fearfully towards this 'political correctness'?

Dare to transgress any tenet of this relative morality of political correctness. If you do, you will be identified (especially by liberals) as a hater, a racist, homophobic, xenophobic, or whatever other epithet that can be hurled at you. The overall aim is to create a climate of fear with the attendant state of being called guilty to complement it—all designed to manipulate and control the individual and ultimately the masses. Do you ever stop to seriously think and reflect upon how so few persons can manipulate and control so very many? Are you among the many? And if so, do you like being there? And if you don't like being there—what are you going to do about it?

This hideous cancer of political correctness continues to grow and metastasize not only here in America but worldwide, in fact, to the degree of altering and in some cases muting your freedom of speech. Soon your very speech may subject you to a hate (speech) crime! Do you not already see that happening?

The propensity for so many in our nation and around the world for that matter to be held captive by the tentacles of political correctness is due in large part to the deep ingraining of one of the various facets of a *basic attitude*, which is at the level of a pathology in many individuals, and all the while, the person remains unaware of the unconsciousness of how basic attitudes play out and the influences they have on the individual's actions and behavior. It may be a *basic attitude* itself that is responsible for a person's inability to challenge political correctness. A person may remain for the most part totally unaware of the source and underpinnings of his or her very own motivations and decision-making processes. And these *'basic attitudes'* have as their underpinning ... the very foundation on which they are created and maintained are the aberrations and disharmonies of the five primary natural emotions! It is upon these distortions in the emotional structure of the individual that serve as the foundation upon which modern-day liberalism is constructed.

At birth, each one of us is endowed with five primary natural emotions. The natural emotions begin to manifest in the activity of each and every individual on earth soon after their birth, and as mentioned earlier, may begin to fully engage as early as six months of age.

The function of the natural emotions, if allowed to work in accordance with their lawful natural design, is carried out independently and irrespective of one's race, culture, ethnicity, or sex (of which there are two—

male and female… just so we're clear about that). This does not mean that races, cultures, et cetera, will deal with the manifestation of the emotions in the same way. They may not, and the differences found in cultures and races are clearly evident. But this does not mean that outcomes and consequences and notions regarding the difference in cultural dealings with the emotions may not be disadvantageous to individuals in a particular race or culture depending on the culturally ingrained attitudes and handling of the emotions and how that plays out.

Nature, nor the individual, does not and will not bend to the capricious whims of changes initiated by cultures, races, ethnic predispositions, or belief systems which, in the scheme of eons of time, are rather short-lived and ephemeral! Nature cannot suddenly just evolve and change to suit the whims and desires of cultures or belief systems, nor change to suit the capricious whims of individuals who have a political agenda, without some sort of natural cause and effect consequence, such as in the same way that President Barack Hussein Obama or Colin Powell suddenly 'evolved' over the course of a year or two on, for example, homosexual marriage, and now, even the Supreme Court has evolved on this matter! And then, this sudden evolution is like a bad virus strain that begins to affect everyone. Now suddenly, as polls indicate, the populace (individuals) is evolving on the issue of homosexual marriage. And one of the emotional drivers towards this 'evolvement' is fear. Many fear opposing homosexual marriage, fearful of being labeled homophobic. This book, however, is not the place to get involved in a lengthy discussion about the sexes. I will save that for another publication that is in the works.

And yes, you may notice, according to recent polls, how just in the last year or two, much of the general public is evolving on the issue. It's often difficult to judge which has the greater affect of influencing the other. Are polls a more suggestive influence to affect an individual's point of view? Or, are the media and those in positions of influence more likely to influence people? The astounding thing about polls, gathered from a very small sampling of the total population, is that those very scant poll results can in turn influence a very great number of the population due to the inherent suggestibility of the masses! Then, at a later date when a sampling of the same suggestible people are polled and it is proclaimed that a change of attitude or belief from as recently as the previous poll has happened, this new basis then is speedily glommed on to by the politicians and the media, so as to position themselves to reap the most in political popularity, notoriety, or monetary gain. This ever-changing ideological tapestry becomes a circular revolving vortex of colliding notions, and one loses sight of whom or what is influencing whom or what. And the concern this should give rise to is whether or not there is anything stable and enduring in our culture and whether or not each and every individual has an enduring and steadfast center of gravity within themselves that will enable them to define for themselves and make up their own mind what constitutes natural behavior or make conclusions regarding some very fundamental principles which guide and govern human behavior—and whether or not there do exist perennial God-given and natural laws!

Do all these gyrations and alterations of changing positions mean that many—and this includes leadership, politicians, the general public—do not have a firmly established center of gravity or belief system within him or herself, and are nothing but malleable weathercocks buffeted by the ever-changing winds of change—and these in turn are molded by polls, pundits, demagogues, or whatever? And one of the main drivers of this behavior is fear, fear of straying away from the herd mentality. If so, then this is in fact a form of slavery. It is a damaging and insidious form of slavery. No one escapes the reach of its tentacles and influence. All are subject to the risk of becoming slaves—slaves to political correctness, slaves to popular convention, political expediency, to the suggestive influence of polls themselves, personal selfish gain, and the backdrop of ultimate control imposed by a growing authoritarian state. And the invisible fences that keep the populace enslaved are the instillation of the cloud of fear and guilt that permeates the psyche of every individual. In the end, it is an abomination as it undermines the very Spiritual foundation of each and every individual. It is sacrilegious to the very core and stands as a violation of human behavior as governed by universal God-given law!

CHAPTER 7

THE EMOTION OF LOVE

It seems appropriate to begin an ordering of the emotions starting with the primary human emotion of love. And really, there is no set sequence or chronological ordering of the emotions, per se, by which they should be presented.

Some of the greatest philosophers, sages, and prophets have attempted to describe love, yet the task remains elusive. It may be easier to define what love is not. Love is not selfishness. It is not to be associated with the selfish need of one to demand gratification. It is not ecstasy—not physical ecstasy. It is not to be confused with ecstasy nor with the erotic manifestations to be achieved with another; however, love may be established by the awakening of these desires. Those erotic experiences by themselves are a manifestation of desire—not love. Love is often confused with uncontrollable and unrestrained desires and behaviors. Often one will make a statement, "I love you." What they are saying to the person is that "You please me—my desires are satisfied through you." But if the pleasure in whatever form it is currently being rendered is taken away, be aware, they may then reject you and even hate you. Love is not suffering in the respect that it has nothing to do with useless suffering which is carried out with the aim to elicit pity, or perhaps to prove one's depth of love by demonstrating a form of twisted and distorted sacrifice or martyrdom; nor is love to be associated with the strict adherence to a form of fanaticism.

A number of words are widely used by many to indicate the emotion of love—*lovable, affectionate, ardor, joyous, tender, fondness, happy, peaceful, satisfied, serene, content,* and *positive.* Love may be considered the highest and most unique of the emotions. Love incorporates giving just for the sake of giving, with no expectation of reward or return favor, and not necessarily as a reactive measure expressed by the term, "You do this for me and I'll do this for you." There is heightened joy and fulfillment in the giving of unconditional love just as in the receiving of it.

By the way, hate is NOT the opposite emotion of love. Hate is a repression and congealing of the natural emotion of Anger, but more about this natural emotion later on.

Love stands alone from the other emotions in that there may be a boundless, if not endless and ongoing outpouring of the emotion of love; whereas, with the other emotions the expression thereof is generally bound to a certain measure and will be in proportion to the associated circumstance which generated the emotion. For examples, with the emotions of anger or grief, these emotions may be expressed in a degree proportionate to the circumstance, that is, an event happens, a response occurs, and the emotion is then expressed. The emotional energy is fully spent and dissipated. The situation as well as the individual directly involved will be free of any repressive or unexpressed emotional factors.

The seemingly boundless outpouring of love may often and readily be witnessed in the eternally recurring romantic displays of two lovers. The archetypal story of Romeo and Juliet serves as a good example. The depth and degree of the love of two lovers appears to be boundless; that is, the giving of love is apparently free of any conditions. In the initial stages there is total love and acceptance on the part of one for the other. Then, as the essences and personalities of each individual begin to interact and blend with the other, frictions and differences may arise to interrupt the free flow of love. This brings about and triggers other emotions of the two eternal lovers or sometimes referred to as *soul mates*. If those other emotions are not dealt with, acknowledged, and expressed, problems may occur that could disrupt the relationship if not destroy it altogether.

It has always been an irony that after a period of time—after the initial idealistic situation of the couple begins to unfold—circumstances happen, things change, and they become bitter enemies, both become embroiled in intense hatred of one another. Oftentimes divorce courts become an inimitable battlefield upon which these events are played out. As it will be said more than once in this book, if the emotions of the individual or individuals are not dealt with properly and become out of rhythm and harmony, certainly within the confines of that relationship—*love* will not flow. Anger transforming into congealed hatred will rule the day.

There need not necessarily be a cause and effect relationship between Love and the expression of it. In other words, there may be no condition of, "I will love you if such-and-such event happens." Or, "If you promise me you will make such-and-such happen, I will give you love in return." If that's the case, then when this bargaining chip is withdrawn, love too is withdrawn, offering proof that this had nothing to do with love. Love may be freely given unconditionally with no expectation of reward or gain; no strings attached, and not be associated or serve in any manner as a bargaining chip, or tool to negotiate certain terms. If there is an ulterior motive behind the giving of love, then I would argue that it is not exclusively love. The driving force behind that exchange may be other factors and other emotions. Only we (ourselves) know if our giving is conditional or unconditional. And by the same token, we also may perceive whether or not the giving of love from another is really a disguised maneuver with the true motive of getting or demanding something of us.

The primary emotions may manifest in the day to day experience of the individual alone are in concert with other emotions. If—and this is a big if—*if* a person's emotions are working in rhythm—proportionality of expression should define and characterize any such circumstance in which the emotions are engaged. This is assuming that an individual is free of any unconscious repressions and repressive pooling of the emotions.

If a person's emotional pool of repressed emotions is not drained and dissipated, then these repressed emotions may infringe upon and embellish the current emotionally charged situation to distort the situation far out of proportion.

Love positively binds us socially to people, connects us to things, people, and to so many other life circumstances; and love allows each person to experience self-love and self-respect. But if a person carries many repressions of the other emotions, the likelihood is that the expression of love will be thwarted and blocked, and will not flow!

CHAPTER 8

THE EMOTION OF GRIEF

Grief is the emotion triggered when a person experiences loss.

Loss may be a part of one's life experience in a multitude of ways. There isn't a single person on this earth in which loss has not been a factor in their experience. It could mean the loss of a loved one due to death or other form of separation, the loss of a job, losing a game, losing an election, losing a loved pet, losing one's ability at physical prowess, losing one's physical looks, losing one's health, and so many other life circumstances in which loss or separation from something or someone occurs.

Grief may be experienced over the unrealized expectation or non-fulfillment of something; the unrealized and unfulfilled potential of vocation, falling short of reaching certain goals, disappointment over the physical body one was blessed with at birth that does not suit one's idealized image of what the perfect body should be like, or falling short of achieving monetary gains. Grief may be experienced by a child over the fact that he or she never had parents, and this grief may be carried for their entire lifetime.

The emotion of grief may occur in concert with other emotions. For example, anger may also be generated in that child who grieves over never having had a mom and a dad. Indeed, the emotion of loss may be experienced in a multitude of ways, and concomitant with that experience of grief may occur the shedding of tears. And grief is one of the (of only two) naturally occurring emotions which will bring forth the shedding of tears naturally. The other natural emotion which will bring forth the shedding of tears is love. Very shortly, this behavioral phenomenon will be discussed further.

It is important to the general emotional health and well-being of the individual that when the natural emotion of grief is triggered, that it be freely allowed to manifest completely to its natural conclusion and therefore be fully dissipated. In the healthy expression of grief—if done to its natural conclusion—an individual moves into a frame of reference of acceptance of the happening, the circumstance, or fact of existence; and henceforth, their life may proceed forward in a positive fashion.

One of the most difficult of challenges for many to overcome in regard to resolving grief—so very obvious, yet so overlooked and readily acknowledged, is the disappointment many experience regarding their physical self; and this includes the physical structure and its unique outer design, one of the four components that make up our total structure. Many Americans look upon their physical body with mild disgust if not outright hatred, to the point of loathing. I've met them and talked with many with such an attitude and perhaps you have as well. Many people become fixated upon an idealized image, oftentimes drawn from those created by Hollywood. The dirty little secret is that many of the so-called *stars* of Hollywood have deep disappointments about their own physical body. Why else would they be so fixated upon their looks? A wise friend once said to me, "Good looks are like money in the bank. Either you have it or you don't. In any case one should accept the reality and move on." But we continue to debate whether or not "All men (homo sapiens) are created equal."

What happens to that grief experienced over something they never obtained? Is it resolved? If the repressions of emotions are not resolved and one moves into a non-rhythmic state of emotional existence, one will be inhibited and blocked from realizing their full potential whereby love will flow uninhibited. If grief is not allowed to manifest in a natural manner, if it is subject to a repressive process—then the repression of grief attributes to the formation of a state of depression in an individual. Only when one accepts fully their physical being in all its ramifications will one move into an attitude of love and acceptance of it for, truly, it is the physical self that houses a facet of the Divine. How great it is when every individual may look upon their complete four component structure which we referred to earlier in our discussion with an attitude of love and acceptance.

An unfortunate pattern of behavior has been established in our culture. It is generally perpetuated from one generation to the next and is characterized in the circumstance when an individual is experiencing grief. A parent or caregiver will attempt to diminish those tears of grief in one by saying something like, "That's okay—you don't need to cry. Keep a stiff upper lip, kid—it's not that bad!" These attempts at squashing the grief process are indicative of deeply held attitudes on the part of parent or caregiver that the expression of grief is a sign of weakness. This is generally an example displayed by those who are uncomfortable with the expression of their own grief experiences, and therefore, will try to diminish its expression in others as this then becomes a projection (commonly called a psychological projection) of their own discomfort they feel. Briefly described, a psychological projection happens when— in this instance—a behavior that one is uncomfortable with, when observed in someone else; the observer will attempt to diminish and downplay that behavior in others.

The end result is that the impressionable young mind learns this attitudinal behavior of grief, internalizes the templates of this behavior making it an automatic pattern of their own behavior—they exemplify those patterns in their own behavior and that behavior gets passed on to the next generation.

Grief is generally always a causative factor and component in Post Traumatic Stress Disorder (PTSD), especially in the circumstances of wartime experiences. In the intense arena of battle, there is no opportunity for the soldier to vent and fully express his grief and go through the normal grief process. Repression upon repression of that grief is taking place. Often in these circumstances, in conjunction with that grief, is the experience of intense fear and anger. When these three emotions are repressed and inhibited, it sets up the conditions to form the rudiments and foundation of PTSD. In any treatment modalities of PTSD, these three emotions must be addressed.

Physically, the experience of grief may manifest itself in bringing forth the shedding of tears as mentioned earlier. Regarding the shedding of tears, there are only two instances in the triggering of the expression of the natural emotions which produces tears. As we learned earlier, the emotions drive behaviors and there are only five possibilities that may be accountable for the production of tears. Of those five possibilities, there are only two; one is from an expression of the emotion of love; the other is from the experience and the expression of grief. Surely all are familiar with how a person may shed tears of joy, as well as how one may shed tears of grief. Any other display and shedding of tears by a person may point to a manipulation and a ploy to selfishly illicit sympathy, to get attention, or obtain a gain of some sort.

It is important to stop at this point and identify this manipulative strategy; that is, the shedding of tears for reasons other than the natural emotional expression. This strategy is learned early by the young child. Most of you have witnessed this ploy. If a child does not get what he or she wants, the child throws a tantrum and cries, whines, or screams until the weak parent, caregiver, or teacher gives in and the child wins by getting what he or she wants. It only takes the child a few of these displays to learn this manipulative strategy, which may continue to be employed well into the lifetime of the individual, even into adulthood. And the parent foolishly gives in to the manipulations of the child, trading some short-lived silence and peace of mind, and the belief that they have helped little Johnnie or Susie overcome their tears—all at the greater price of creating within the psyche of the child a lifetime of dysfunctional behavior for that child. I ask you, dear reader, "Was that a fair exchange?" And yes, this strategy learned by the child and employed by some is symptomatic of modern-day liberalism. Indeed, liberals regularly are given to whining and complaining, and an occasional scream, all in an effort to illicit attention.

This behavior, in its rudiments, has the characteristics of extortion. This form of behavior may also manifest without the presence of tears. Just because tears are not present, does not mean the behavior is not grounded in the same behavioral dynamic. How often do you witness a liberal using tactics of threats, screams, demands, and manipulations to achieve an end—tears or no tears? Hillary Clinton frequently is on the giving end of screaming episodes in an effort to manipulate and control, to achieve an end. And there are many who will weakly and fearfully give in.

A frequent example is that of the Reverends Jesse Jackson and Al Sharpton demanding that various businesses or corporations purge themselves of discriminatory practices; otherwise, if those businesses don't comply, the Reverends will extract a pound of flesh from them, And this pound of flesh generally takes the form of money.

The same tactics are supported by many of the liberal leadership. Both President Barack Hussein Obama and Eric Holder perpetuate the belief that extreme racism is inherent in our culture, even if the citizenry has no conscious awareness of it. It is due to this presumed inherent racism that blacks have been held back from achievement in life. In fact, these liberals are creating an artificial construct of grief, and it is on this construct that they will justify their actions to coerce, control, and demand. Usually a sizable chunk of money miraculously cleanses and heals the situation. Remember, behaviors are driven by emotion. These ploys are driven by repressed grief, fear, and anger. The use of emotion, though distorted, is in the driver's seat—and has high-jacked reason, facts, logic, and reality.

As the child grows into adulthood the tears may subside but the manipulative strategy remains intact. Those kinds of tears are not based upon a primary emotion. This trait may remain with the person for a lifetime and yes, as said, it is a liberal trait. I have seen it and so have you ... politicians shedding tears not because of an intense emotion of love or grief. In these cases, it is a sign of character weakness, not a sign of strength. It may be a manipulative strategy and attempt to elicit pity ... pity me ... look at me ... poor me! Or they may have a belief that by shedding tears they prove themselves to be a sensitive and caring person. Do you want these people in elected office representing you? Do you want these people in positions of leadership? No. Likely you'd prefer they go to some sort of therapy. The next time you see one of our elected officials crying in the House or Senate chambers of Washington, DC, whether it's John Boehner, or whoever, evaluate where those tears are coming from.

Recently, in January, 2016, your president, Barack Hussein Obama, when delivering an impassioned press conference in which his major focus was whittling away at your Second Amendment rights, displayed tears running down his cheeks. These tears had nothing to do with grief or love, but rather, these tears were fake tears … crocodile tears. This was a ploy and a manipulation on his part to get his way. It's a safe bet it is the same ploy he used as a child to get his way by manipulation of his parents and grandparents. Dear reader, do not allow yourself to fall into this trap of Obama's manipulation. Obama is impassioned with the desire to take away your guns even if he has to shed fake tears. Why? You must ask yourself why. On the heels of the terrorist attack in Southern California, which has spurred the upsurge in gun sales by the citizenry because they feel vulnerable and want to be able to protect themselves, Obama wants to inhibit you from owning a firearm! What is the good sense of this?

If one of our elected officials is shedding tears of love and joy over an awe-inspiring celebration of a Fourth of July parade eliciting an intense emotion of their love of America, then we can understand and accept that. Or, if one is shedding tears of grief during the Memorial Day ceremony commemorating those who gave their lives to preserve our freedom, we can accept that as well. But if those tears do not originate from an experience of an emotion of love or grief, do you think this behavior could be revealing a manipulative liberal predisposition and perhaps the situation needs to be evaluated?

Maybe they're just shedding crocodile tears. You've heard of the term crocodile tears? This notion implies that the tears are fake tears. No doubt, the tears are fake, but what has been lost from that ancient notion is that the real cause of these tears is produced from pressure applied to the crocodiles tear ducts from devouring sizable prey. Crocodile tears are fake tears in the respect that they are not triggered by emotions, and also for the additional reason that as we learned earlier, a crocodile being a cold-blooded reptile and different from the human and mammalian species, has no emotional component. It was not created with an emotional component. These crocodile tears shed by individuals when there is no valid emotional basis for those tears equal cold-blooded manipulation.

CHAPTER 9

THE EMOTION OF ANGER

The third primary natural emotion we'll examine is the emotion of anger. It has been proposed that anger is the most misunderstood all of the natural emotions despite the fact that all of us express the emotion numerous times during the course of every day of our lives—even though we may not realize the great extent to which we do.

Anger is the emotion that helps guarantee our very survival as it is very much a part of the instinctual survival drive. Anger is the natural emotion that propels us to initiate positive aggressive behavior to move against obstacles in life, to help us take on all the various challenges we encounter—whether to ward off the least and the most benign attempts of others to impose their will upon us, or to withstand more aggressive forceful moves against us by manipulative despotic individuals attempting to assert their will upon us in authoritarian nation states. Anger essentially propels us to hold our ground—whether it is to defend our character, defend our property, or protect and sustain our God-given rights. Anger is the emotion that compels us to hold and assert authority in the defense of maintaining our pride and self-respect and maintain our sense of well-being. Anger is the emotion that compels all Freedom Loving Americans to defend the Constitution of the United States of America, especially when it is clearly evident that our Constitution is under assault by the liberal and progressive elements in our society!

But when the expression of anger is thwarted and repressed, the energy collects—becomes congealed, distorted, and coagulated—and becomes a cauldron of hostility, rage, and hatred just below the level of consciousness; and then when linked with and augmented by fear and guilt (guilt such as one internalizes from a relativistic false morality as often instigated by political correctness), it becomes a very destructive force. We may witness this behavior continually almost every day as humans regularly unleash this destructive force to viciously attack their political opponents by the use of destructive lies, or to the extent to kill one another. Humans, in many respects are no different than the mammalian species (though mammals do not kill other mammals out of repressed hatred). Considering the exceptional fact that humans (potentially) have reasoning; one would think they have the ability to live a rhythmic life and allow their natural emotions to guide them into a rhythmic, positive, and productive life. But the evidence bears out that any natural quality that becomes distorted becomes a negative and destructive force to the individual. Anger when allowed to manifest in proportion against the current circumstance we happen to be in, serves to bring balance to this cause and effect circumstance of our lives, and therefore may then be viewed as a healthy emotional discharge and characterized as positive behavior.

Does anyone not think that our Founding Fathers and the early colonialists were driven by intense Anger over the usurpation of their rights by the British Crown? Of course they were, but anger was not the only emotion that was engaged by the colonialists on the road to the establishment of our great country! Their choices and behavior were driven by other emotions working in concert.

Our Founding Fathers did not suddenly get this notion that they 'feel' everyone should be entitled to Inalienable rights. No, not at all! Rather, they as individuals and among themselves reasoned that all Mankind are granted by their Creator, certain Inalienable Rights, and among those are life, liberty, and the pursuit of happiness. They fashioned their position from the work and perennial beliefs of many others who had preceded them. When they observed that these very rights were under assault, they were intensely angered. "Give me liberty or give me death", as Patrick Henry so eloquently stated in his famous speech, was not based upon a whimsical 'feeling'! It was driven by intense Anger! There was nothing wishy-washy about his position... there was no threat to 'draw a red line in the sand'; rather, it was concise and affirmative.

We've identified how the emotion of anger can move and propel one to action—to move against obstacles. Anger, by itself alone—when engaged in proportion to the circumstance, moves us to constructive action in opposition to the challenge at hand. But anger should not be the prime mover and motivator to solely carry us forward to the ultimate conclusion of the envisioned goals and dreams that we aim for. Anger may be augmented by other of the natural emotions due to the natural emotions often working in concert.

Reinforcing the point again to reiterate that the expression of anger needs to be in proportion to the circumstance—proportionality is a key ingredient in the natural expression of anger. If an individual learns that the expression of anger is a negative behavior—that individual may instead repress anger rather than express it in a natural fashion, and that would be in opposition to proportional expression. The repetitive and habitual repression of anger can only result in adding to an unconscious pool of repressed anger, which over time, intensifies and congeals, forming the basis for intense hatred. If one houses within themselves a seemingly boundless pool of repressed anger, that anger becomes a seething caldron of negativity and hatred. Upon discharging that hatred—whether the precipitating event for that discharge is based upon some real-time event, a learned inculcation of a belief or ideology, or upon an imaginary event—it is as if a dam suddenly burst and much pent up energy is suddenly released! Then, this disproportionate destructive behavior and discharge cannot build or create, and lead to anything positively constructive—it can only destroy. Then, as generally happens, upon examination of the precipitating event which triggered the anger—there is not found one single element of proportionality; nor is there generally found any thread of rationality or reason upon which the violent discharge may be justified.

The repressive and congealing process of anger which ultimately results in the unleashing and discharge of repressed anger and hatred may result from two causes; one, from an intense discharge of congealed and repressed anger which has been compacted into one's unconscious because that individual has learned in their life experience to fear anger, and therefore, they avoid, deny, and do not express anger; and two, from regular and systematic subjugation by the inculcation of teaching layer upon layer of hatred which may (and will) one day inevitably burst forth. Witness the terror, destruction, and mayhem currently perpetrated by the ISIS (Islamic State). They are driven by intense anger and hatred which has been drummed into their psyche; hence, they do not build anything, but only destroy! They destroy people and cities; they hate and destroy Christians and destroy traces of Christian cultural symbolism which they believe does not synchronize with their fanatical ideology. The ISIS is driven by fanaticism. Their fanaticism is so narrowly focused that they even kill their own religious affiliates. As mentioned earlier, the roots of fanaticism are grounded in the relentless inculcation of ideology and in distortions and repressions of the primary emotions. All reason and logic has been blotted out by this extreme fanaticism.

There are a number of words in our vocabulary—often used interchangeably, and dependent upon the degree of anger one happens to be experiencing when one is expressing or describing their emotional state of anger. These words are more accurately identified as intellectual constructs and notions that are often used to describe the state of anger one may happen to be in. The following words may be used to describe the state of anger, to name a few; *rage, ire, wrathful, hostile, livid, infuriated, enraged, incensed, mad, disgusted, frustrated, exasperated,* and *irate.* Underlying these constructs is the one constant—anger.

Regularly used if not overused in expressions by many in the media is to state that they are 'frustrated' about a certain issue, circumstance, or event. Turn on your TV and especially watch the news casts as they discuss news events. Often you will hear the word 'frustrated' associated with an event—an event that should in reality register high on the Richter scale of emotions… as intense anger! Just today, I had the TV on and heard the word 'frustrated' again. But do they call it anger?—no! I've heard the word used by military generals, elected officials, potential political candidates, and others in authority. Let's be clear about this. There is no such stand-alone emotion as 'upset' or 'frustrated', but there is the emotion of anger. Frustration is what the little old seamstress experiences when for the last five minutes; she has unsuccessfully tried to thread the minuscule eye of this needle. She may say she's frustrated but what she is really saying is that she is angry. There seems to be a deep resistance on the part of many to acknowledge that they are angry and then stating in no uncertain terms that the emotion of anger exists.

When someone says, "I am really upset about that!"—or, "You really upset me!"—or, "I am very frustrated!"—or, "You frustrate me very much!"—what are they really saying? In the least make a simple acknowledgement that they are angry. Okay, now the question becomes, what are you going to do about it?—express your anger, or as many do, challenge it or the person who 'made' you angry? It is totally wrong-headed to believe that someone 'made' you angry. Or do you repress your anger and go on your way sulking and seething, complaining to all you meet up with what a complete bastard so and so is for making you feel that way! This last option is generally the pattern of behavior of one who has learned to repress anger for the reason they believe the expression thereof is a bad thing. If this forms the basis of one's belief system, this becomes the foundation of so-called passive-aggressive behavior. The person cannot express their anger freely and proportionately at the moment of the circumstance so they repress it. But the energy of the repressed emotion must (and will) eventually find an outlet. So the individual goes about their daily business allowing the poisonous repressed energy to fester in their unconscious, and in a gradual process the negative energy seeks and finds an outlet and consequently taints so many of their daily encounters in life due to the disproportionally of expression. Habitual and repetitive behavior patterns of this kind will generally identify that person as having an *attitude*. Remember what we talked about earlier of how attitudes are formed.

The fact is, no one makes you feel anything, but rather, you choose to feel whatever it is that you feel. It is a typical liberal trait and a psychological projection to direct blame of problems on various sources that always lie outside of one; it is someone else's fault, you made me feel that way, et cetera. In the United States of America, the liberals are solely responsible for turning our country into a blame oriented society. It is they who are responsible for shifting responsibility away from certain individuals, institutions, or things, and deferring the blame to whomever or whatever they deem should bear the full brunt of responsibility. The liberals have turned our nation into a blame-oriented nation of fault-finders. The fault and blame always rests upon or within ... someone else, an institution, the lack of a law, someone's failure to act, past deeds and circumstances, et cetera. But never, as far as the liberal is concerned, is the individual to blame, unless, of course, the person happens to be a Christian conservative. Political correctness gains strength and momentum due to this distorted belief and mind-set. Liberals believe that if they can sanitize words, actions, people, and life circumstances, then the conditions will be eliminated that cause people to feel bad.

On the flipside of this distorted viewpoint, liberals look to people and things outside themselves to fix the cause of the problem. And be assured that liberals self-appoint themselves as the ones to fix the problem. Therefore, (and so they believe) we (liberals) are going to alter institutions, things, and people to make the world a better place whether you like it or not! It is your (the non-liberal) fault, and you!—need to change to make the world a better place, and we're going to see to it that you do and we will set the rules for you! We, the liberals are going to see to it that the people!—need more rights and protections, and only bigger government, more regulations, and more laws to establish equality are going to fix that, et cetera, and we're going to see to it that it happens! And amidst all this, you may query, "And this is supposed to be the land of the free"?

As mentioned earlier, all of our actions and behaviors are driven by emotions—emotions of which either acting alone or in concert with other emotions are expressed countless times on a daily basis. Anger is the emotion that may move us against the greatest of challenges, and is also the same emotion that drives our simplest of actions, such as saying No to the least little thing! "No thank you, I don't care for another bon-bon" as the host passes around the dessert tray of those fattening bon-bons!—the same bon-bons of which the host toiled for hours to make just for you. And the host spares no words to let you know that fact and will relentlessly push them on you and may at the same time (unconsciously) heap guilt upon you for having the audacity to say no! Go ahead, dear reader, despite all of that, you may go ahead and say no comfortably.

Don't be confused or misled into thinking that the expression of the emotion of anger may be identified and classified as anger only when it is displayed as this violent vehement discharge of emotional energy. To accurately identify the emotion of anger, you need not necessarily always look specifically for this kind of display at all, though, of course, it may be displayed as such, if the circumstance warrants it. Again, the key is whether or not the triggering situation and the resultant emotional response are in proportion! And how does one gauge and measure proportionality? Remember this; in those situations when you instinctively know you are fully in charge of the expression of that emotion—chances are, you are expressing that emotion in proportion to the circumstance. And after that discharge, if you feel guilty or remorse about it, then you may need to open the door for some personal introspection.

Yes indeed, that simple response, no, is driven by the emotion of anger. Have you ever met someone in life who just cannot say 'no' to anything or anyone? Sometimes they are referred to as 'yes' people. There are some people who just cannot say no when that tray of bon-bons passes their way. Why is that? And in their most private moments they confess to you, "For some reason, I just cannot say no." Do you think that person may fear their very own anger and aggression? What is it they're afraid of? Do they refrain from saying no for fear they will be disliked? Does guilt play a role in this behavior? If the person says, no … will guilt ensue? Will any expression of anger in any magnitude of expression by this person generate guilt? Indeed, to simply say no, does engage the emotion of anger. Then, considering the psychological dynamics of that individual—when a circumstance arises which would under normal circumstances illicit a great degree of anger; then that same individual would be incapable of expressing anger in a balanced response to the situation.

Did you know that to say no comfortably, is concomitant with one's ability and comfort in asserting authority? To say no to the simplest of demands or requests placed upon you by others is in effect a gauge of how one may maintain authority over oneself. If one cannot assert authority to maintain autonomy over oneself, then just as certain they would be uncomfortable asserting authority over others. Do you remember studying coefficients in school? A coefficient you may recall was a constant value. What is your coefficient of anger? Do you have a high or a low coefficient of anger? Hopefully it is not '0'. There is a direct correlation with one's coefficient of anger—and how they serve in a position of authority.

If you find one in a position of leadership, whether an elected official, manager, or corporate CEO, who is out of rhythm in the expression of their anger; they are most likely very ineffective, authoritarian, dictatorial, becoming rage-full, or showing a display of anger way out of proportion to the circumstance. A very simple gauge to determine the effectiveness of an elected official, manager, CEO, et cetera, is whether or not they have the capacity to display reason, logic, and common sense—and not use violent displays of anger as a management tool, through the use of punitive coercion, threats, or various forms of manipulation.

In another manner, if one has an ingrained attitude in regard to the expression of anger in that the expression thereof somehow indicates negativity of behavior, then if accused of being short-tempered, they may likely cave to the criticism, such as what recently happened to Rand Paul amid the events surrounding him while announcing his bid for the presidency of 2016. What did he do? When accused of being 'short-tempered, he says sheepishly to the liberal TV reporter gal Savannah Guthrie, "Yes, I have to get better at holding my tongue and holding my temper"![1] The act of holding one's temper is synonymous with the predisposition to repress and suppress anger, or of having an incorrect attitude about the expression of anger. Rand Paul, why not get angry and feel good about it? When our country is being transformed and changed by the liberals before our very eyes and directly under your noses (and speaking of noses, especially by one, Barack Hussein Obama, who looks down his raised nose with an attitude of disdain for you the citizen)—this should register the greatest of outrage and anger by all freedom loving Americans, and certainly by you!—and towards one who aspires to leadership of our country! We do not need the type of person in positions of leadership and authority who will be intimidated by liberals, or doesn't have the capacity to show righteous anger! In your life and experience, you have undoubtedly heard of someone who has a bad temper or is short tempered as if that person were born with that predisposition. No one is born with a bad temper; rather, that predisposition to behavior is a learned trait.

When Rich Lowery commented on FOX following that exchange between Paul and Guthrie, he remarked, "Anger must be used sparingly." What! Are you kidding me, Rich? What does 'sparingly' mean? Is there only so much to go around? Is anger a scarce commodity? Is this sort of like Obama's pie of wealth?—when he says, "There are only so many pieces to go around." Bull crap, Rich! Have you any idea what you're talking about? You're absolutely wrong on this one; anger should always be used in proportion. There is more than enough reason for all Americans to feel righteous anger for what is happening to our country. This is just another example of backing away and denying what should be a natural proportional expression. And judging from the hysteria of these media gals, Rand, I'd say you fell a bit short. Anger is the emotion that gets us propelled against obstacles and resistance. When will you people realize that our country is undergoing a destructive change and transformation; our Constitution is being dismantled, our Judeo-Christian foundations are under attack, our military is being decimated, our borders may as well be non-existent, our free market economy is disappearing, and our three branch system of government has been hijacked by the judicial and executive branches!—can you not get angry? If you can't, I'd say there is something very wrong with you.

Ann Coulter, on the same FOX segment says something to the effect, "The candidate should not get into the angry exchanges—leave that to the attack dogs on your side of the campaign!" Wrong Ann—this is nonsensical and wrong-headed! The American people want to know who the candidate is! The American people respect a candidate with fire and passion! People respect those who can demonstrate authority and passion—not those who are weak, timid, and withdrawing. When will you pundits learn this and get it indelibly imprinted into your psyche and head? Take a lesson from Donald

Trump. Why do you think he is leading comfortably in poll after poll? It's because he has no fear of speaking his mind which includes, the expression of anger. Obviously, there are many people who resonate well with that, and on some level they know, understand, and respect that it is part of our natural predisposition. Surely, it has to point to something very fundamental to our natural being and behavior. Why can't you all get it?

On another much greater and widespread scale of activity, we have some of the so-called conservatives in the House of Representatives—leaving aside for the moment the lost souls of the Democrats, Republicans, and RINOs who find it impossible to engage their anger and say no to the many liberal agendas proposed by the liberal President and the many other liberals found throughout the House and Senate! What is it they fear? Is the American electorate content to have a Congress and Senate full of fearful individuals? For one to have the ability to say no with no residual fear and guilt, forms the basis of our natural aggressive abilities. You, dear reader, gave your full vote and support to these many elected officials (countless liberals regardless of party affiliation) with the understanding that they would act in full authority to carry out their sworn duties, the most important of which was to uphold and protect the Constitution of the United States of America. If they don't follow through, then you were sold a bad bill of liberal goods ... in many, if not all cases! Yes, you were lied to, but you bought into it!

Are we being much too hard on these elected officials? Are our expectations out of line in expecting them to be more aggressive? Of course, there are times when submission and acceptance must be practiced, and aggressiveness must be laid aside, but the notion that both of these abilities within an individual, that is, in the proper time and situation, to be able to demonstrate submissiveness or aggressiveness are somehow mutually exclusive—is an erroneous notion. Submission need not have anything to do with a perception of weakness. And to be overly aggressive is generally a compensatory act serving to mask and cover over various dynamics in the individual's personality that is based in fear. If one's ability to be both aggressive and submissive is in balance, one may comfortably be on either the receiving or the giving end of the words, "No thank you," without experiencing any residual fear or guilt. All depends on whether or not one's emotional structure is operating in balance. Distortions in this balance may prevent one from practicing positive submission, because in a liberal mind—that would be perceived as a weakness. Submission to a liberal is much too fearful an exercise.

By the way, it is well to mention here that ALL the natural emotions are positive, but it is my perception that the natural emotion of anger is viewed by many in our nation and culture in a negative way. Open your dictionary and look up the simple definition. You will discover that in no manner is anger defined as a positive emotion. You will generally find it defined something along the lines of annoyance, displeasure, hostility, wrath, ire, or rage. Anger is naturally designed to be employed for the best of service to you, but your dictionary will certainly not define it as a positive natural emotion.

You may be aware of 'anger management' classes—generally prescribed for those who cannot control their anger and who are identified as given to angry and rage full outbursts. The emotion of anger, in like manner of all the emotions, is created in us as part of our instinctive machinery, and to a great degree, all emotions work autonomously involuntarily in a reactionary manner producing responses that ultimately augment our behavior and are the drivers behind our choices. So, by a narrowed definition, anger cannot be controlled in the strict sense of the term, just as many other of the naturally occurring functions in your physical, mental, and psychological being and body cannot be controlled. But an individual may assert a repressive influence at the onset of anger. Then, as the repressive influences continue and patterns of behavior become fixated—anger, if not expressed rhythmically will begin to congeal within one and internally envelop a person as a repression. And then in the flow of life circumstances as they happen, anger will discharge autonomously in ways and in circumstances of which a person may be unconscious of the source and foundation from which is produced the motivation to anger. The repressed anger then overrides conscious choice and is then actually in the driver's seat—so to speak—and will control you!

One may apparently choose to repress anger or express it to a degree after its onset, but in our highly complex society it is neither always expedient nor possible for one to freely express anger depending on the situation one is in. One must then determine how and when to express anger at a more appropriate time, but it would be more advantageous to do so as promptly as possible. There is great wisdom in the Biblical injunction; *Eph 4:26, "Be angry, but sin not; let not the sun go down upon your anger."*[2] And why should this matter? It is because unexpressed and repressed anger carried over from today to the next day and the next, collects in the pool of repressed anger, and this dammed-up energy will eventually force an outlet—but the risk then is that the expression may be far out of proportion to the then current circumstance. Or the discharge of this energy may occur in a circumstance having no relationship to the initial formation of that anger—and the expression thereof in that context will generally contribute to our detriment as well as to those in our surroundings.

After the onset of anger associated with an incident, one may learn to repress it and deny it. This is the equivalent of trying to put on a lid and cap off a source of pressure or force, and sooner or later, it may blow with a violent explosion depending on the magnitude and degree of the repressions and how those repressions configure with the circumstance. And indeed, should a persons' congealed anger manifest as intense and violent hatred resulting in bodily harm to another—then yes, there are consequences for that act. The notion of controlling anger before it suddenly comes upon one and therefore must be controlled, is an erroneous notion! Remember what was said earlier about the differing volatility of energy used for thinking compared with the energy of the emotions which operate with energy of a much greater volatility.

The foundation of the child's early learning experience regarding anger during the formative years—generally learned from the parents—is that anger is a negative behavior. Under these conditions, the child expresses anger—and what does the parent do? The parent may react with anger and then exacts punishment upon the child for 'getting angry'. Why punishment?—because the parent learned and internalized a specific attitude and belief about anger, that it was bad negative behavior. Instead of learning to express anger rhythmically and naturally, the child learns to repress it in the same way the parents did, because after all, a parent only knows and can instruct either by word or action (example), only those templates of basic attitudinal patterns of learning that have been deeply ingrained within their own psyche.

Therefore, the attitudes are set in place whereby the child fears anger, and it makes no difference whether anger proceeds from them, themselves, or from others. An expression of anger from themselves may likely result in guilt, or the expression of anger from others may trigger fear. In those emotionally charged situations where anger is present—they will likely cower, retreat, or attempt to gloss over those situations. The simple reason a person will fear anger is because they were told as a very young child that expressing anger was 'bad' and to express it makes them a 'bad' person. In addition, when scolded for expressing anger, the state of being called 'guilt' is established in the psyche of the child. Furthermore, because some parents would physically punish the child for the expression of anger—the prospect of punishment added to their fear compounds and reinforces the prohibition. This sets in place in the psyche of the child—the predisposition to fear anger, and hence, even the simple inability to say no.

When the expression of any of our natural emotions are repressed or thwarted by ourselves or by an outside authority or agency, the emotional energy becomes repressed and dammed up. The expression of any of the emotions should ideally happen in a proportional balanced manner. If someone inadvertently or willfully... the reason really doesn't matter—cuts you off in traffic, you may loudly yell, "You *#&%@$ s.o.b!" But you do not attempt to run them down and force them off the road, do you? Well, some do! So-called road rage is a display of repressed anger; it is not a proportional response to that specific situation which just occurred. If one's emotions are balanced and working in harmony and proportion—you would not choose to aggressively run someone off the road if suddenly cut off in traffic. Would you utter an expletive or two? Of course, but run them off the road? No. You would utter an expletive or two and the emotion would be spent.

What happens to the very young infant or child when he or she is slapped around and abused by the parent or adult? Parents and caregivers carry out this practice based upon the justification that they are 'disciplining' the young child. At some level of understanding in the psyche of that young child, he or she unconsciously knows that their self-respect has been violated, and surely in some manner of instinctive understanding in that young child—anger is stimulated! Then, the question must be asked, "What happens to that anger of the young child?" Obviously that anger remains unexpressed. If as an adult, suddenly in some unexpected life situation, you were physically slapped and punched by someone—what would you do? Wouldn't any self-respecting adult become angry as hell if slapped around? Would you resist and fight back? We should all hope so! Should the desire for self-respect be of any less import and bearing in the existence and experience of that young child, as it is in the adult? Added, a child is more governed by instinct than by conscious thought. Remember this, when a violation occurs to disrupt the operation of lawfully functioning instinct and then following is a disruption and inhibition of that naturally occurring instinct— that occurrence will not be free of consequences.

If the child becomes angry in defense of himself (the response of which is an instinctive natural and unconscious response) against the abuse of the out-of-balance adult, then this show of resistance of the child only solicits more slapping and abuse from the parent (because the parent justifies his or her behavior on the premise that they are disciplining this unruly 'bad-tempered' child), and this sets in place the process of the child repressing even more anger out of fearful retribution by the parent. The parent justifies their behavior toward the child by saying, "By gosh! I will beat the unruliness out of this child, if I have to—to straighten the kid up!"

So begins the repression process. And sadly, if the chain is not broken—this predisposition of behavior is passed from one generation to the next. This is where the notion originates from, that is, of the sins of one generation being inherited by the next.

It is only years later—drawing from the example above of the abused child, that we hear of this—now young adult—walking unto a schoolyard in Stockton, or a movie theater in Colorado, or another place or city in America—brandishing a firearm and begins to mow down any person who gets in the way. And those who personally knew the young adult will say with shock and surprise, "But he was such a good little boy, just kept to himself, never said anything ... very reserved, never got angry at anyone, et cetera." But he was emotionally repressed and the day came that all those repressed emotions, along with other contributing factors, were set off resulting in this misfortune. And in this instance as in many similar to it—you do not blame the firearm for committing gun violence, nor do you file suit against the firearm manufacturer as if they are to blame for the act! The firearm is not the source of the problem and neither is the manufacturer. The individual still must take the responsibility for his actions. Should parents, teachers, and caregivers be held culpable for the behavior of that child? After all, they are responsible for a great part of this conditioning. No, not really ... can't hold them responsible certainly not lawfully. There are no laws in our society against the manifestation of stupidity and ignorance, per se. But in our contemporary society, there is a shift away from posting blame (responsibility) on the person who actually commits the act—unto factors outside of the perpetrator ... parents, institutions, the firearm itself if not the firearm manufacturer. The predisposition in our culture to establish blame and guilt runs very deep. This is the grossest of projections on the part of individuals in that the blame for missteps is always outside of one. This is rooted in a foundation of fear and guilt and must be expunged. In other words, a person is not responsible for much of anything, the cause lies outside of one ... so the liberals would have you believe. Hence, when the liberal is apparently the cause of an issue or problem—the liberal too will sidestep the responsibility and a long string of excuses of the behavior will follow.

But the repressed emotional energy bound within each individual cannot remain repressed forever, and sooner or later it must and it will find an outlet. Nature is very exacting and efficient in that in all its natural systems, nature strives for balance and equilibrium. The repressed energy bound within the individual at that unconscious level cannot remain static for long ... it will find an outlet. These things are governed by natural law. Within the human species—very much is governed by natural instinctive law.

If a body is invaded by a virus, the body will induce a fever state to kill the virus, thereby striving to maintain balance and optimal health. If a body ingests a bacterial invader, illness will ensue, and the body will instinctively organize its internal defenses to rid itself of the germ. If a body is cold, the outer portion of the body will shiver in an attempt to move warm blood to the outer surfaces of the body to stabilize the body temperature—along with, of course, conscious efforts are made on the part of the individual to find a warmer environment. Both conscious and unconscious mechanisms are in place to help achieve a state of equilibrium in the individual. Another good example of this unconscious mechanism perfectly represented doing its work—is of a person long imprisoned and starved of food. A specific subject matter of night time dreams of this person may be that of sitting down to a bountiful meal and thoroughly enjoying it! Upon awakening from that dream sequence, the satisfying effect experienced by the dreamer in that dream sequence continues in the awakened state and consciousness of the dreamer. Though ephemeral—upon awakening—a satisfying affect is produced in the consciousness of the individual which may linger throughout the day and even beyond that. Thereby, the dream sequence offers a counter-balancing effect to offset the conscious reality in which the person is living, in this instance the condition of starvation.

Another example of the body striving for equilibrium happens if a human body does not get a sufficient quality in the food eaten; the body will (unconsciously) demand more intake even if by sheer volume of food in order to extract the needed nutrients demanded by the body. It is as if the body is 'communicating' to the person at a very cellular (unconscious) level that it needs nutrients. But the consequence of one submitting to the unconscious demands of great volumes of food generally results in obesity—and all the negative health ramifications that come from ingesting not only the great volume of food, but if the food happens to be of an inferior quality. In these situations in which the person does not get food in sufficient quality, a condition of perpetual hunger ensues which in turn stimulates this over-consumption of food. Again, an example of how nature strives for balance. Those of you who have spent a sufficient amount of time in farm and ranch country will know that when the livestock were lacking minerals and nutrients from their feed, they would literally begin eating the wood fences. Why? At an unconscious level their body needs and demands nutrients. So what did the ranchers do? They conveniently placed for consumption these purple-ish and red-ish blocks of mineral salt which the livestock thoroughly enjoyed and received a health benefit. They didn't dare feed the livestock the mostly inert white refined salt. No, that is reserved for humans. What did we say earlier about mammals?—they are more attuned to their natural instincts than we humans are. I recall kids in school who would sit in the classroom and chew their wooden pencils. If you should witness this happening, have the parents consult with their physician. Perhaps what the kid needs is a good dose of trace minerals, as the common diet today is extremely lacking in such, given the propensity to overindulge in fast foods and Twinkies. In my experience I have found that a generous introduction of quality sea salt will help solve the problem.

Hopefully, these few examples just given may serve to fortify the notion of how the natural predisposition of the human body and psyche is always directed to a striving for balance and equilibrium.

This inherent striving for balance and equilibrium applies as well to the emotions. If the emotions are out of balance due to repressions; the body will strive for balance by trying to discharge the dammed up emotion. If the emotions attempt to assert themselves into the realm of thinking, the domain for which they are unsuited, then thinking and reasoning becomes lop-sided, distorted, and faulty. And as we are learning, when so-called 'thought' is directed via the influence of the emotional component, which is the primary foundation of 'liberal' notions; reasoning and logic becomes shoddy and unreliable, if not totally non-existent.

It is also a fact that the repression of emotions also has a detrimental effect on the physical body, in the respect that various organs of the body may be detrimentally affected. Remember, the emotions are a form of energy within the physical body. Hence, why do we have the expression, *worried himself sick*. Worry is from the emotion of fear... fear, turning and turning inside one will literally make a person ill.

Do you really believe all those protestors in Ferguson, Missouri, were discharging all the anger and intense hatred only over the shooting, and this is assuming they had a keen impartial intellectual grasp of all the facts surrounding that shooting? Of course they weren't. They didn't care about facts because their thinking and reasoning was not engaged. And even thereafter, once the facts were revealed and the facts did not conclude in their favor—this made no difference to them. And even if the facts of the circumstance had of unfolded as they claimed and worked in their favor, does this synchronize or provide balance (or an excuse) to justify their behavior? Again, the answer is no, as these circumstances only served as an opportunity they grabbed on to for venting their hatred and destructiveness. And sadly, the rabble in Ferguson, Missouri was supported by the liberal cheering section led by the likes of Al Sharpton, Eric Holder, President Barack Hussein Obama, and others.

What we saw discharged from the protestors in Ferguson was an eruption of the pool of repressed emotion (hatred) of all those persons. All those repressed emotions of those individuals had everything to do with their own personal psychology and internal factors created from their individual experience in life; developmentally, environmentally, and psychologically. And by the way, the many protestors who were bused in from the surrounding areas who really had no hate-the-racist-cop axe to grind, saw it as an opportunity to get paid by the promoters who were agitating the hatred—to earn a few bucks in the process, and make off with stolen goods and merchandise from the destruction and looting of the businesses! They too were driven in their behavior by their own generalized hatred and anger.

In this extremely volatile situation there was an absence of reason, lack of attention to facts, or the application of any logic!

To add a different perspective for the purposes of contrast—is anyone aware that Tea Partiers who by and large, self-identify as conservatives, were present at these protests ... looting and destroying property?

For that matter, are there any instances, anywhere, of Tea-Partiers or conservatives burning, looting, and destroying property?

Many of the Ferguson, Missouri protestors— overly emotionalized—were incapable of engaging their reason, logic, and common sense. So, what do these protestors do to compensate for their lack of these things? They resort to displaying placards with three or four word mindless slogans written upon them, accompanied by their hysterical shouts, and vent their poisonous emotion by the burning of police cars, assaulting police officers, and by the looting, burning, and destruction of others property.

From the highest leadership in our land and down the hierarchy to the local levels in Ferguson, and including many others of the same bent—all used the rioters as pawns in their own selfish destructive game in the midst of these circumstances as a means to vicariously vent their own pent-up and repressed hatred and festering anger held against America. Did those in leadership just mentioned step forward to condemn the actions and call for the enforcement of our laws, which were clearly violated? No, many did not—and why not? Because they, in like resonance using the metaphor of the tuning forks, identified with the rioters. They too identified with the four or five worded slogans written on the placards.

Yes, anger may be taught, and the inculcation of it will result in congealed hatred, relentlessly hammered into the impressionable child by parents, teachers, and caregivers. It need not necessarily result from something that happened personally, physically, and psychologically to the individual, but may be inculcated none-the-less and learned in a vicarious manner.

The many young children in Islamic countries are taught beginning at an early age to 'hate' Jews, Christians, and the West. With enough drumming into their psyche, it becomes a festering pool of emotional hatred. Even by the time they are entering adolescence—which by the way—is generally the time that one's spiritual facet may begin to awaken and blossom; instead, rather than their spiritual facet opening at the onset of adolescence, they are ready to lash out and kill ... even the young innocent impressionable children are ready to strap on the explosive vest and walk into the crowds to kill, even though the children never had any direct contact with any of these three groups mentioned, towards which their intense hatred is directed! Surely, don't you think these actions are the grossest bastardization of any notion of spirituality or religion?

Mr. President, Barack Hussein Obama, where did you learn your indoctrination and anger for America, which has been festering for many years, and in my opinion, turning into a seething hatred? We can readily observe the chronology of the indoctrination of young Islamic children ... but what about you? You made it clear at the beginning of your terms of election to office that you wanted to fundamentally transform America. Why would you want to fundamentally change and transform America unless you held a deep-seated contempt and hatred for America? At your inauguration swearing-in, why did you bumble and fumble in your pledge to "protect and uphold" the Constitution of the United States of America? Do you remember that?—you and judge Roberts. Instead, you turned it into a joke of sorts and many laughed! Was there no room for solemnity? Do you possess any love at all for this country? Is there any love at all that flows from you in support of this country?

Did it begin with the tutelage of your grandparents sponsoring and initiating your early indoctrination by the communist and sexual deviant, Frank Marshall Davis? Or was it maybe your long time minister and mentor, Reverend Jeremiah Wright ... remember him and those many sermons you heard over a twenty year period, famous for expelling his venomous hatred, "goddamn America"! This is who you are, President Obama!

Then, there was President Barack Hussein Obama's' Islamic sponsor and advisor Khalid al Mansour. For the record, there are numerous layers of events, validating how Obama's support both financially and ideologically, stems from wealthy Saudi Arabian oil barons with close ties with those supporting black nationalism, socialism, and communism—and this would go full circle to include, Frank Marshall Davis. And the list would be lacking not to include your friends, Bill Ayers and Bernadine Dorn, having engaged in their decades-long violent acts of extremism aimed to hurt and kill? Whatever it was to cause the behavior displayed from you—surely all of the above made a generous contribution which you readily internalized. Mr. Obama, you became beholden to this socialist anti-American doctrine with roots reaching well into Islamic doctrine. Why else would you bow to a Saudi prince on foreign land? Mr. Obama, why do you regularly go abroad and condemn and criticize America? Why would you accuse Americans of having no ability to build ... whatever?

It is the same indoctrination of the very young such as what happened with children raised in the homes of the Ku Klux Klan, in which they learned to hate blacks. Is there any difference between this and the young children of black families growing up in South Chicago, or any other city or suburb, in which the children are taught to hate whites with a passion?

Happening today in Oakland, California, is the indoctrination of young girls. They call themselves radical brownies.[3] Don't be fooled by their claim of fostering 'social justice', whatever they imagine is contained in that absolutely silly stupid two-word slogan.

Their true intent is to spread hatred against white cops who they claim are indiscriminately killing blacks. And these young girls are being brainwashed by their parents, teachers, and care-givers to learn hate. That's right—as said earlier, hate can be learned, and they are learning to hate! Those irresponsible adults are inculcating these strong damaging suggestions—suggestions of which bypass the critical sensor of the conscious mind of the young girls, and implant directly into their unconscious mind, thereby becoming the basis of future hate filled behavior.

I carefully watched the videos of them. These young girls present themselves as heaving not a thread of reason or logic—which reasonably at their age cannot be expected of them—but instead, are well on their way to growing this venomous hate which is metastasizing within their psyche—as the inculcated anger builds and grows only to become repressed and poisoned. Even the brownies berets are modeled after those of the radical hate group, the Black Panthers.

As stated earlier in this book, as one becomes laden with layer upon layer of learned anger—congealing into hatred ... add to that equation an intense fear (learned by repetitive inculcation into their psyche by parents, teachers, or caregivers) ... that is, fear of policemen, especially white policemen—the resulting sum total demeanor and attitude of that young girl on her way to becoming an adult—when in the presence of a police officer will display an undercurrent and attitude of negativity, hatred, and distrust. Hence, any police officer, white or black and who is street-wise and accomplished in the art of reading people, will readily perceive the demeanor and hatred exuding from that individual and the officer may in fact assume a cautious and defensive manner and mindset. Those young girls of Oakland will grow into adulthood carrying this negative attitude, and I want to lay great emphasis on the word, *attitude* as we discussed earlier! An *attitude* is accurately reflected by—and it betrays the fraudulent façade that has been superimposed onto these young girls—their inner emotional condition, which creates the breeding ground for negativity. In Muslim countries in which the young girls are taught to hate, the ultimate step in their indoctrination is to strap bombs onto these young girls and direct them into crowds of innocent people to kill themselves and others. What is the next step all of you in Oakland have in mind for these young girls? What constructive—if anything, do you expect to come out of this?

This unfortunate scenario was enacted in the circumstances with Michael Brown in Ferguson, Missouri. Michael Brown presented as a young man filled with hate and anger which he displayed against the white cop. This is what I mean by having an *attitude*. Remember what was said in an earlier chapter about *basic attitudes*.

The subjugation and brainwashing of these children who as of their current age, do not have the life experience nor the capacity to engage in self-directed logic, reason, and common sense—whether of this race or whatever race or nationality, or the children in Oakland or in Islamic countries—in these different circumstances is nothing short of a horrific crime! This is nothing short of bringing these children under subservience and control by those in authority. Dare we use the word enslavement? Hence, is this why it is written in *Matthew 18:6, "And whoever misleads one of these little ones who believe in me, it would be better for him that a millstone were hanged on his neck, and he were sunk in the depths of the sea."* Surely, the use of our children solicited to serve as pawns—as an extension of the psychic distortions and aberrations of those in authority to further their own ends is a horrific moral crime!

A political action committee ad that was run in late 2015 by liberal Democrats during the Republican and Democratic nomination campaigns used young children as principle actors in the ad, with the purpose to smear Donald Trump. This situation contained elements which were no different than those employed to manipulate the kids in Oakland. These kids displayed the most intense anger and profanities—profanities totally out of sync with their age and experience. The young kids did not have the life experience, knowledge base, or wisdom of *being* to know what they were doing. They were manipulated and used as pawns by those adults in authority. This too was a shameful act perpetrated by those adults in charge. There is a likely chance these kids will grow into adulthood carrying this intense hatred as a result of the brain-washing imposed by irresponsible dysfunctional adults.

The many children across America who are being subject to the same indoctrination (brainwashing) of hate America mindset in like manner as the children being brainwashed in Oakland, will be the next generation of protestors who make a presence at the next accidental and uncalculated clash of individuals which ends in the death of someone. They will be there spewing forth their pent up and repressed venom and hatred—learned those few short years earlier … the mode of expression via their four or five word mindless chants and slogans uttered by the collective in a mindless mechanical fashion. And of course, absent from such an environment filled with distorted poisonous emotion is any reason, logic, or common sense. But you may count on the liberals being there to use it as an opportunity to further their agenda…

"Can't let a good crisis (opportunity) go to waste"—the quote made famous by the Rahm Emanuel, and fully supported by his close colleague, our current president, Barak Hussein Obama. This has to be the basest and grossest of human behavior, using these circumstances to further their own twisted agenda. Should we not monitor closely what's happening in our schools in America of how the young children are being taught to revise our history ... setting in place the predisposition to hate America? Are they not being taught that our country was founded upon hate and greed? Are they not being taught to hate Christianity? Is this any different than what Hitler did with the German youth?—that is, indoctrinate them into the Nazi way of hatred, beginning this indoctrination at an early age.

Many of the placards carried by protestors in Ferguson were not constructed by the very protestors but rather by outsiders. In like manner these same protestors were again used as pawns by those on the outside who held greater authority and control over the impressionable participants. These same people on the outside carried the same psychology as the protestors, i.e., much pent-up and repressed anger and hatred. The mindless pawns were spurred on by the press, and placards were provided by those outsiders of like psychological bent. These are the same misfits supported and encouraged by the liberals, just to name a few, President Barack Hussein Obama, Attorney General Eric Holder, and Reverend Al Sharpton, and all the many more liberal supporters who subscribe to their distorted ideology, many of whom occupy the halls of the Senate and Congress. And as I mentioned earlier, there is no capacity on the part of these people to be introspective and self-examining.

In a climate of affairs such as what unfolded in Ferguson, there is an absence of reason or logic. The protestor's justifications for the behavior of which they commit is of a most distorted foundation. Because of the fact that they indeed discharge some of their pent up and repressed hatred and emotion, they therefore believe that because this reckless venting makes they feel better, and they indeed experience a semblance of cathartic effect, artificial though it is—is justification enough for them to continually commit their heinous acts. But they are only projecting their inner problems unto the outside of themselves, making everything and everybody, especially the police, the cause of their woes, and therefore wrongfully attacking them. Introspection is not one of their stronger suits.

A wise teacher and friend once said to me, "Make anger your friend." But in order for anger to be your friend—it must be expressed in proportion to the circumstance, and then … you are in charge of it—you direct it in the manner you choose which would be constructive and not destructive, and indeed only then is it your friend and companion. Otherwise, congealed and repressed anger and hatred will control you and unleash autonomously as if of its own accord—will generally be expressed far out of proportion to the circumstance and can only lead people and events into negativity and destruction. The question often arises, "How will I know that I am expressing emotion, in this case anger, in a balanced proportion to the circumstance"? You will know because you will have no sense of lingering animosity in that situation. You will be free of it. When the pool of repressed emotions (anger) within you has been drained away, you will be free of them. Then, as it reads in Matthew 5:39, *"But I say to you that you should not resist evil; but whoever strikes you on your right cheek, turn to him the other also."*[5] This verse often leads to misunderstanding and is directly responsible for many of the notions of non-violence that periodically crop up. It makes no sense that if someone strikes you on the cheek to turn the other one. Why? So you can be stricken on that one as well? That's foolish. What is that supposed to achieve? Rather, the verse is conveying to one to foster a proper attitude. If one has developed the proper attitude necessary to turn the other cheek ... then, to have the capacity to turn the other cheek means that one is free of repressed anger. The verse is not to be taken in the literal sense. If someone strikes you and commits an aggressive act against you—you have the right and the responsibility to protect yourself. But as will be said more than once in this book, only when your emotions are working in balance and harmony, and you are free of emotional repressions, only then will love flow.

Anger, a naturally endowed emotion is designed to serve us in a positive way. But culturally, we have made anger our adversary, and those who express anger—even in a natural manner—are often viewed with disdain. The key to making anger your friend is that it must be expressed in proportion to the circumstance. Then it becomes your ally and your friend with the goal to assist you to move against any and all obstacles in life.[4]

Human resource departments across the country are falling victim to the dark cloud of political correctness in that expressions of anger by a person may identify and stigmatize the person as a hostile individual. This is nothing short of a distortion and a manipulation of the natural human emotion of anger and the natural expression thereof.

---

[4] *During the writing of this book, on 1/29/2015, a FOX News segment with Megyn Kelly presented a clip of Senate hearing with ninety-one-year-old Henry Kissinger present. Code Pink was there displaying their usual placards with catch phrases on them, accompanied with their usual one-liner rants and shouts. John McCain, to his credit (and it's seldom that I agree with John McCain) angrily with voice tempo, (paraphrased) "demanded that they shut up and get their scum out of the room!" Kelly's two guests (one liberal and one conservative), Mark Hannah, and Marc Thiessen, both chided McCain for his heated response to Code Pink and accused him of "dropping down to their level."*

This is a sample of the B.S. the media feeds the people! What the hell are they talking about? Dropping down to their level!? McCain was exactly correct! I would like both these guests to fully explain what "dropping down to their level" means. Maybe both would like to "take a timeout and lets engage in a dialog" and give a hug to these idiots, Code Pink! This simple illustration is a representative microcosm revealing a deeply ingrained mindset and attitude within our culture that somehow the expression of righteous anger is a negative. We need more natural expression of anger. As often repeated in this book, the proportional expression of anger is a positive! Far too many in our culture reject anger, deny it, and fear it, even fearing their own anger and the expression of anger from others, frankly, its unhealthy behavior.

When saying the word, hostile, say it with a great deal of feeling and verve. Doesn't the accentuated pronouncement of the word hostile have much greater impact than to just say angry? It's as if the word hostile conveys the flavor of criminality! In a linguistic manner, doesn't the word hostile convey more dreadful force than the word anger?

Many of the American Indians were labeled hostile, which gave all the more reason for them to be decimated and removed—as in the example from history—indigenous Indians were removed from Georgia to the then barren fruitless land of Oklahoma, in what became known as the trail of tears. Hypothetically, compare the two following military orders if issued to the cavalry, and determine which carries more force?—"Go attack the angry Indians"—or, "Go attack the hostile Indians?" The fact is, the Indians were extremely angry for being removed from their land and thereafter decimated, so they fought back! Wouldn't you? In contemporary America, a nation that is an enemy of the United States is not deemed angry—rather, we describe these enemies as hostile! And I am not bringing up these two examples from our nation's history to discuss the rightness or wrongness of those decisions, but simply to explain and emphasize a point. Now, any American citizen who may express anger, even though done quite righteously in a natural manner, may fall into a small separate class of those who are hostile! But don't count on this segment of the population as being placed into a protected class just because they happen to be a minority. Rather, in this instance, this particular minority will be discriminated against and likely attacked.

Then, to make matters worse, even if expressing a garden variety of anger, you will be labeled as one prone to (and you may have heard the term)—that is, prone to predictive violence. While it is true that efforts have been stepped up by business institutions, social and educational institutions, and police departments, et cetera, to curb workplace and other violence, and to pre-indentify those who may be prone to violence, thereby preventing violence from happening beforehand—it is unfortunate that caught up in this web of surveillance may also include those who are the least likely to commit brazen crimes reaching the level of assault and battery. With the advent and growth of the internet and social media, and the growing sophistication of screening tools and software, almost anyone may be subject to what I call 'emotional profiling' as even spoken words may be sifted from the sweep of information—designating one as prone to violence, and hence, acquiring the label of hostile! You are now guilty of a thought or word crime! When this happens, off you go to the nearest re-education (anger management) facility.

Human Resource departments will be on high alert to detect and report even the least indication of anger. Those same department personnel are motivated in great part by fear, should they be accused of negligence and lack of vigilance in reporting—thus, opening the door for them to fear liability issues or get terminated from their job. Hence, the most innocuous and benign signs of anger may be reported. Though one may be comfortable in the expression of their anger, and the expression thereof may have been in proportion to the circumstance—it is as if even a spoken word will automatically predispose that one's next behavior will result in violent activity. This is absurd and only contributes to a cloud of fear hanging over all the citizenry.

Upon an examination of the myriad of beliefs and mindsets which seem to be ingrained within our culture—the belief apparently deeply rooted, is the belief that anger continues to be viewed as a negative behavior. Fostered from such a belief is the creation of an environment which can only result in further repression of anger—the repression of which can only have detrimental effects upon the individual, the family, and the society. Repressed anger cannot remain contained in the person's unconscious and sooner or later it will break forth in ways that will be out of proportion to the circumstance and may be very destructive to all involved. But when this happens—what is the response of the collective populace? They proclaim that so-and-so has an 'anger' problem, or has a 'bad temper', never understanding the dynamics at work. Therefore, anger is the problem and the collective soon subscribes to this belief. As is so common today, some prevailing beliefs—even though totally distorted beliefs—held in common by the collective soon become entrenched in the realm of political correctness. The result of this political correctness then sets in place a heightened vigilance of the populace—many then positioning themselves in readiness to detect anger and emotionally profile those very persons whom they consider guilty of such expression. This in turn causes very many, should they be accused of displaying anger, to further repress their own anger—the exact opposite of what should be happening in order to establish healthy rhythmic behavior in the individual.

Do you recall the following circumstance in the campaign season leading up to the presidential election of 2008? John McCain was accused of being a very angry man and due to his volatile behavioral outbursts, many found working with him very unsettling and disagreeable.[6] Remember how the press got hold of this psychological predisposition and behavior of McCain's and criticized and condemned it, and demanded that if he wants to be a likable candidate, he needs to change and stop his angry behavior and uncontrolled outbursts?

So what happens? It was obvious that McCain made an abrupt change. You might perhaps recall this. Thereafter, in a noticeable way he became namby-pamby and lost his anger and his passion! Remember the TV news clip in the '08 campaign of the gray-haired lady asking McCain about Obama because she could not trust him and suspected him of being an Arab?[7] Rather than aggressively getting on the offensive and telling the truth, McCain says in a very sheepish fashion, "No, no, no ma'am, he's a decent family man citizen that I just happen to have disagreements with on fundamental issues..." Despite the fact that by that time, surely McCain—as many in the public and private information sources had already learned or suspected of Barack Hussein Obama's socialist and radical leanings; his association with the likes of Bill Ayers, the Reverend Wright, and so on. Does anyone really believe that by that time, John McCain was not well aware of the vitae (or certainly aware of the lack of an evident vitae) of Obama and of his many questionable associations? By doing what he did, McCain missed an opportunity to be honest, show some righteous balanced anger, and to demonstrate positive aggression and genuine leadership.

We the people don't need namby-pamby's in our political offices. We need people with passion—people who can get angry as hell to get things done! Do you think for a moment our Founding Fathers were namby-pamby? Of course not, they were angry and passionate! We need people in our halls of Government who can get angry, as well as people across our nation to get very angry about the disasters perpetrated by officials in the halls of government of our own country! Our Constitution is being dismantled and destroyed! We have an authoritarian president who, despite what you may believe, is driven by fear and repressed hate and distorted anger—who is decimating the precision balance necessary in our three branch system of government, by usurping and directing authority into the executive branch. Does that not stimulate great anger within each and every one of you? Do you even know and suspect it is happening? Are you paying attention to it? If so, do you care?

Passion, by the way, in the context of which it is so often spoken of in the public arena, is representative of three main emotions; *anger, jealousy (zeal), and love.* Earlier in this work when discussing the metaphor of the gardener, I talked of the synthesis of thinking, reasoning, and planning; coupled with the driving force of emotion to achieve his goal. Likewise, did our Founding Fathers get this wishy-washy fleeting notion that, "Oh hey, we feel like we have these inalienable rights and the Crown is not treating us fairly and therefore, we need to call a time-out, draw a red line in the sand, we will get to the facts, and engage in some measured and controlled dialogue—and it may take some time and not happen overnight, but we will get it done." I don't think so. Nothing would have been achieved!

Rather, our Founding Fathers and many of the citizenry were fed up with the over taxation, lack of representation, and the mandates and controls imposed by the English Crown. The Founding Fathers carefully and methodically formulated their goals and ideals— fashioning their aims amidst much writing, dialog, and debate. The accumulation of their goals and ideals were gleaned from many perennial sources of philosophical, theoretical, and theological sources—all having stood the test of time and human experience; gathered from many sources to include Biblical teachings and precepts, universal laws and perennial principles as set forth by Locke and others.

Our Forefathers, understanding how the common rights of 'we the people' were denied, and power was usurped by the English Crown ... their emotions stimulated them to action. Yes, they were intensely angry at the Crown of England for the many instances of top down control to which they were subjected. Those colonists, envisioning their goals, were driven by anger and furthermore motivated by jealousy and zeal to achieve those goals—and then rendered those goals and ideals to written form. In the current Democratic pre-presidential debates, I heard the candidate—the older gentleman soon to be prime material for fossilization, Bernie Sanders remark, "Our forefathers were not driven by anger and fear." The old man has not a clue. It was for the love of their country and the envisioned prospects of self-determination—ultimately leading to the creation of freedom for all the individual citizens. Their goals were so important that many were willing to lay down their life to achieve them. Of course they were angry!

Did they experience fear as well? Of course they did, does anyone think not? Can you imagine engaging in this conflict knowing you may face losing all your property that you toiled and labored a lifetime for—and worse, not knowing whether you and your family could be rounded up and shot or hung for what was then considered by England and the Crown, a treasonous act!

But rather than back down, they moved forward despite their fear... they challenged it! Is there anyone in Washington, DC today who would have like courage to stop the decimation and destruction happening to that very same Constitution that our forefathers were willing to lay down their life for? Does anyone actually believe that Hillary Clinton, who it appears, will be the front-runner on the Democratic side for the presidential run has any qualification what-so-ever to do the job? Far too many of the elected officials occupying the halls of Washington, DC, are more concerned about their legacy, getting re-elected, protecting their fat and bloated pensions, protecting their private health care, and growing and solidifying their many DC connections to fulfill their selfish aims and reap increased monetary gain especially once they leave office. They don't fear what is happening to this country; their greatest fears include losing those things just mentioned, or straying away from or being booted out of their big 'ideological tent'.

All fears within a person—only with the exception of two, are learned. Any fears that one learns—may be unlearned. How many of the elected officials in Washington, DC, are capable of unlearning their fears? Do they even desire to? How many are really courageous enough to do what it takes to turn things around? Few, if any … most of their concerns are directed at themselves because most are inherently selfish people.

Fear is like a two-edged sword. Fear is the emotion that when augmented by other emotions may stimulate one to take on the greatest and most monumental of challenges, even in the face of death: and fear is also the very same emotion that may cause one to cower and retreat from not only the greatest of challenges, but from the most innocuous and benign of challenges, or to retreat in fear when one's selfish desires are elevated to greater importance than the survival and longevity of our Republic! Where does the degree of fear rank in magnitude—especially in those instances where one's selfish greed and self-interests are elevated to more importance than present and long-term National interests of the people for whom they were elected to serve? Wherever that ranking of fear may fall, I don't hold much hope, if any, that even a few would challenge it! So what's the answer? You, the citizen need to participate. Don't allow yourself to fall into the role of practicing the ostrich syndrome, which is, sticking your head in the sand and then pretending that all is well. Learn the facts and learn who the elected officials really are, learn what they stand for, learn how they vote or if they vote at all (recall what we said earlier about absentee votes), subject all what you have learned to sound reason and logic; and if what you conclude about them does not measure up to high standards... engage some passion—pay attention, take action, and boot them out of office by your vote.

CHAPTER 10

THE EMOTION OF FEAR

F ear, the fourth primary human emotion, is the natural emotion designed primarily for our self preservation, and in the most basic manner, assists us in our very survival.

At birth, constructed within the structure of the emotional quadrant is the emotion of fear. We are born into this world possessing only two natural fears. Those two fears are the fear of falling and the fear of loud noises. The basic utilitarian design of these two fears is to help assure our survival. All other fears which may manifest from one's life and experience are fears learned during the life experience of the individual.

It is primarily during the first seven years of the life of the individual that the foundational templates of learned fears are constructed. It is very important to grasp the essence of what was just said. Review and read again what was just stated—born with only two fears— let that notion sink in. Only two fears—**all** other fears are learned! This is a very powerful statement!

There are numerous other words in our vocabulary that indicate the emotion of fear: *anxiety, apprehension, ambivalence, trepidation, tense, nervous, pensive, stressful, concerned, confused, indecisive,* and *insecure,* to name a few. But all of these descriptive words created by the mind and intellect as part of our vocabulary are really just words that we use to describe experiences based upon one primary emotion. All of these words—no more than intellectual constructs—essentially do the same task and that is, point directly toward the foundation of that one primary emotion—the emotion of fear.

Burst a balloon in the presence of a very young child. The loud burst triggers that primary inborn emotion of fear and the child will automatically show a look of surprise and possibly cry. Stealthily approach an adult from behind and pop a paper bag and they will jump in surprise. A sudden drop or fall of a child will solicit a look of surprise and fear on the child's face. The experience of an earthquake stimulates the basic fear of falling. As we discussed earlier, mammals, too, possess this same inborn fear. Some kids get a curious kick out of tossing their cat into the air and observing how it manages to right itself in free fall and land on its feet. But while in free fall it is flailing about with claws bared with a look of abject fear on its face. The emotion of the fear of falling has been triggered in that cat. Your dogs and cats also take a leave of absence on the Fourth of July during the loud reports of the fireworks displays.

It is early in one's life experience in which the process of learning various fears begins. It isn't long before the young child begins to learn various fears. Let's posit that if you took a young child to the zoo for the very first time and allowed that child to crawl uninhibited and unrestrained into and through the retaining bars of the wild animal cages and among the wild animals—animals of which that child had not yet accumulated any life experience to form associations and learn fear of the animals—indeed, that young child would not experience fear, at least, not until the animal growled loudly or took a swipe at the child, knocking it down. The child was not born with the fear of that wild animal. Then, guess what? Never again would that child crawl freely into such a cage. The child just learned a constructive lesson, which is to fear those wild animals!

Things of this nature may set the stage for the formation of various phobias in the psyche of that child. But as the disclaimer goes, all of you at home, please do not try this with your child on your next visit to the zoo. Furthermore, you don't want Child Protective Services knocking at your door. This one simple lesson of learning fear, though rudimentary, is an example of how fears are learned, and in this instance, the learned fear satisfies the aim and need of self-preservation.

The dynamics of an individual's fight or flight instinct are grounded in the basic stimulations of fear. It is fear which augments our decision making as we begin to learn our capabilities and to set our limits of when to challenge a threat or obstacle and launch head-long into it, or upon evaluation of the circumstances under the scrutiny of reason and logic, back down.

But the sources from which so many individuals learn to fear are multitudinous. Learned fears may serve to sustain us and trigger our basic survival mode, or fears may serve to cripple and stifle us to inactivity. This stifling to inactivity (or contrary-wise, exaggerated disproportionate reactions to circumstances) may be exacerbated when the emotion of fear becomes severely distorted, and these same distortions are compounded by the concerted effect of other emotions which are out of rhythm.

In addition to the learning experiences gathered from the physical environment, the child learns (both consciously and unconsciously) all the various psychological and personality traits of the parents, caregivers, and those in positions of authority. Indeed, the earliest most dominant environmental factor of conditioning that has the most influence on the child is from this very environment of those standing in authority, foremost is that of the parents, that is, a Mom and a Dad. The child is exposed to myriad personality and behavioral traits of the parents and caregivers who, in effect, project by word and action their own psychological makeup and predispositions. Whether they are overbearing, overly cautious, fearful; if they have more extreme characteristics of a predisposition to be punitive; if they are sadistically inclined or are physically abusive; parents, caregivers, teachers, and those in authority are the primary sources of conditioning from which the child learns various fears. Parents, teachers, and caregivers, teach kids to fear based upon the simple fact that all the various deeply ingrained basic attitudes of any person in a position of authority may be projected onto the children and internalized.

Compounding the installation of fear into that young child, the early formative years of the child are much more conducive to the emotional hard wiring; that is, the propensity of this hard wiring to become indelibly ingrained into the psyche of the young child.

Those early years set the stage and begin the formation of the many emotional templates of fear. Make no mistake, many fears we learn help assure our self-preservation, but when fears become magnified and distorted, we have countless people across America who are riddled with anxiety to the extent that anxiety is classified as a disorder in the professional mental health nomenclature. But the causes of that anxiety are generally not specifically named; rather, the anxiety is based upon generalized factors that need to be explored and revealed. Anxiety stems from the instinctual primary emotion of fear. There may be a host of reasons why people across America are anxiety-ridden.

There are many conditions of our experience that may trigger the natural emotion of fear. To possess a learned fear of something does not automatically mean that the fear is doing us a disservice. As we grow and learn from the many conditions of our existence, we accumulate myriad experiences and learned activities, many of which will be modified or augmented by the emotion of fear. Fears, and that includes learned fears, may serve to maintain our safety and well being. On the contrary, learned fears may serve to cripple us to inactivity, depending upon how we learned that fear and the foundation of it.

In a manner, it's a very liberating if not comforting thought; that is, that we are born with only two fears. Therefore, we need not go through life with all the many fears compounding and turning within us, fears which do not serve us in a positive manner. It should be a liberating thought to know that we have a choice with regard to the attitude we form with regard to various things or events that we encounter in life, whether of events that happened in the past or of events from present circumstances. We have a choice of whether we wish to continue to fear them or not.

Many in our society ingest countless medications for anxiety disorders. Unfortunately, medications only address and anesthetize the symptom, but do not neutralize the basis and cause of the fear. Anxiety is fear. All the many fears and anxieties that we learn can be unlearned. How is it then that it seems so many individuals are burdened with so many fears in our culture and in our world?

Physiologically, we do ourselves a disservice when we become overburdened with distorted fears and anxieties. In our current times, it seems that fears and stress levels are extremely raised. When a person exists under heightened levels of fear, the adrenal glands are forced to increase hormone secretions. From these constant demands of hormonal production, the inevitable result will lead to adrenal gland fatigue. This then results in a number of physical disorders, including digestive disorders, heart disorders, high blood pressure, metabolic irregularity, chronic fatigue, and depression, just to name a few. Does anyone believe that a young child or a person of any age is exempt from these same physiological consequences? I say no! The full emotional functioning of that young child is fully engaged very early in the child's life.

These principles of the human emotions here outlined should have been a part of Head Start. Who was it who started Head Start? Bush? As it is, they're missing a key ingredient if they don't know this. And I ask you, dear citizen, do you really think you need or want to tolerate the fear generated by political correctness imposed upon you?

Fear is generally experienced physiologically in the gut. Actors, athletes, performers and such, experience butterflies in the stomach. This is simply a low-grade fear experienced before the event as slight adrenal secretions begin.

You've heard or used the phrase, "I have a gut feeling." But to add clarity to this phrase, the question needs to be asked: from where does the 'gut feeling' originate? The pronouncement, "I have a gut feeling" is generally applied wrongly. Fear is generally experienced in the lower plexus or gut. An intuitive feeling or hunch is generally perceived from the spiritual quadrant and not from the gut. If the intuitive message we receive is associated with something we should practice caution with or if it stimulates fear, then one does in fact feel fear—one has a gut feeling—yes, from the gut and indeed it is a signal to the individual to use caution.

This phrase applied to any circumstance not involving fear is a misnomer. For example, if you say, "I have a gut feeling my lucky numbers will win the lottery," this is strictly intuitive and not necessarily associated with fear originating as a gut feeling, unless one has a reason to actually fear winning the lottery. But why would one fear that? Maybe they fear many will come knocking on their door demanding money. Then, it's more accurate to say, "I have a strong intuitive feeling I will win the lottery," a strong intuitive hunch.

Unnatural and distorted fears are what shift us out of the present moment of experience and may keep us mired in a regretful state of existence in the past, serve to distort and create apprehension in our views and planning for the future, and consequently keep us engaged in endless worry. And the reason for this is because the basis of so many fears originated from a past experience, and that unconscious past fear will, by association with the present circumstance, inevitably rear its ugly head to shift us out of the present moment. Constructive attention to the present along with creative planning for the future will be disrupted by these intrusions into our present consciousness of those past experiences.

Preoccupations with the past shift us out of the present moment and create the conditions for worry. Worry is a distorted and learned fear. Generally, we worry about what will happen or not happen, we worry about this, or we worry about that, worry can become endless. If we were free of emotional distortions, and this includes distorted fears, our positive and proportional emotional resources along with our reason and logic would be focused on the present challenges which we would then meet in a positive manner. Then the path becomes much clearer for making well thought out plans for our present experiences today as well as for the future. As the guiding biblical injunction succinctly reads in Matthew 6:34, "*Therefore do not worry about tomorrow; for tomorrow will look after itself. Sufficient for each day is its own trouble"*.[1] If we are free of distorted fears, we could practice this injunction to the fullest, and our attention would be laser-focused upon the challenges currently at hand, augmented, of course, by other natural emotions hopefully working in rhythm.

But when fears based upon past experience and repressions color our present moment, our troubles compound and overwhelm us. It is this backward-looking propensity that keeps us mired in fear and in the past. Remaining mired in distorted emotions also prevents us from opening fully to experience the emotion of love which is a necessary step to re-uniting with God from where we came. As it reads in Luke 9:62, *"Jesus said to him, "No man who puts his hand to the plough handle and looks back is fit for the kingdom of God."*[2]

When one becomes burdened in life with many repressions of anger and fear, their overall demeanor and state of being is affected. They may often present themselves in their daily interactions as very negative or down or depressed people, and then again, as a compensation for these attitudes, they may augment how they display themselves with the opposite of these characteristics in their behavior, that is, with a façade and show of arrogance or overbearing behavior.

You have met them and so have I. They present this underlying current of anger, but not so readily observable is fear. Often, it is repressed anger coupled with fear that causes them to lash out at the least provocation. What should manifest in the individual as natural positive aggression becomes distorted into overbearing behavior and over-aggressiveness. Some, as a defense mechanism, create a false mask of power on their outer persona, often presenting themselves with an additional mask of a strong personality, but the real purpose of which is to hide their many internal fears and anger. This sort of defense mechanism has nothing to do with asserting positive authority. Furthermore, when in the presence of such a person, evaluate how reason, logic, and common sense play a role (if any) in their interactions. Generally you will find that their behaviors are driven by raw, distorted emotion, often totally lacking in reason, logic, and common sense.

Think of the many people in the public eye— those in the media and so forth. Does it sometimes seem that they carry this undercurrent of anger, negativity, and fearfulness, seldom smiling or exhibiting a sense of humor? Stop for a moment and consider all the following people quite visible in the media and in the public eye and reflect on the demeanor they generally display and whether or not they are capable of genuine heartfelt laughter.

Following are just a few to observe, but don't stop at these: Al Sharpton, Nancy Pelosi (except for her occasional fake laugh and strained smile), Jeremiah Wright, Supreme Court Judge Ruth Bader Ginsburg, Mitch McConnell, Elizabeth Warren, John Boehner (cries more than he laughs), Joe Biden (except for his occasional silly sophomoric laugh such as he exhibited at the 2012 presidential debates), Harry Reid, Hillary Clinton (except for her occasional disdainful and hideous laugh) John McCain (except for his occasional Elmer Fudd-sounding laugh), Reverend Jesse Jackson (has anyone ever reported a sighting of him engaged in heartfelt laughing or smiling?), Michelle Obama (have you ever witnessed her genuinely and warmly laugh and smile? As much as we know, by her own admission, she scowl-fully hated this country until as recently as '07 or '08), Chuck Schumer, and many others too numerous to mention. Have you seen them genuinely engaged in laughter and joviality out of heartfelt humor? Laughter, by the way, is sometimes known as 'life's best healing medicine' and originates from the emotional quadrant and is of the primary emotion of love. Liberals by and large, do not have very much of a sense of humor. That's why you don't see them laugh very much; and furthermore, that may be a reason so many liberals are so easily offended, because many don't have a sense of humor.

Those people immersed in negativity avail themselves as good candidates to rally around, but by whom? Like tends to attract like. Many are drawn toward the plethora of negative headlines of issues that tend to grip and hold the attention of the masses. It is because they closely identify with the various circumstances—they resonate emotionally with them—and this allows them an opportunity to vent and discharge some of their repressed fear and anger. They feel rather comfortable and at home in such an environment of kindred people as indeed—in the very least—a semblance of cathartic effect is achieved in their collective venting process. They find easy justification for their actions because it feels good. But, as it reads in Proverbs 14:12, *"There is a way which seems right to a man, but the end thereof are the ways of death."*[3] In gatherings of the masses who are immersed in such negativity—who are often engaged in one of the many protests that we witness—nowhere is reason, logic, nor a grounding in factual information to be found, but rather, the proceedings are driven by those unified and consolidated together by the distorted and repressed emotions of fear and anger.

Those in positions of power and authority who have at their disposal the means of the bully pulpit and the media—learn to use their own (and others) repressed anger and fear as a tool of manipulation, especially against those who are lacking in inner fortitude, inner authority to resist, or the inability to apply sound reason, logic, or common sense to counter against it. And added to this equation, many of these same people who are targeted and vulnerable to all sorts of manipulation, for the reason that they may also have an unconscious fear of anger—anger necessary in asserting themselves against it, are now rendered powerless. Furthermore, fear prevents them to act against it and in the final analysis all factors make them likely candidates to fall victim to this manipulation.

All people, regardless of socioeconomic status, race, culture, sex (and here we're talking about male or female, the only two true sexual orientations in this earthly existence), profession, or station they occupy in life, carry within themselves fears of some sort or another. No one is free of fear. Very many of our actions and activities are influenced and augmented by fear. An infusion of fear into an activity may be very subtle. In a given situation, a fearful person may not necessarily present the most obvious body language that would betray a fearful reaction. And then again, fear may exhibit itself in a person's behavior in a vehement, pronounced display—fully accompanied by the exaggerated wide-eyed look of shock and surprise characteristic of a show of intense fear.

All of us, if asked if we have met or know of anyone who we would claim is fearless, we may say yes we have. But, are they really free of fear? Some of the most celebrated actors and actresses on Broadway and Hollywood, who you might think are the most confident fearless people in the world, have admitted of their paralyzing stage fright before each performance— the fear which never in their long career subsides.

The accomplished skydiver, though appearing extremely confident and at ease after hundreds of jumps, nonetheless, never sheds that twinge of fear before each jump. The fighter pilot before embarking on that mission—is he fearful? Yes, of course. Would the tight-rope walker performing his act suspended high above the crowds find any benefit in completely ridding himself of fear? Of course not. To do so would jeopardize his very drive to use caution and maintain his safety.

One may never get rid of fear. We may challenge a fear that stands between us and the achievement of a goal or objective as we strive to overcome obstacles, but we may never be completely rid of that fear. If it were possible to totally get rid of all fears (even the organically based foundation of the emotion of fear), remembering that the emotion of fear is necessary to engage our survival mode—it would actually pose a threat to our well-being and our very existence.

But when one is overly laden with fear, another curious phenomenon happens. This phenomenon about to be pointed out is readily observable in the behavior and interactions of a liberal.

Liberals, as we have learned, feel their way through life. And yes, fear is an emotion that plays a big role in directing the behavior of the liberal. When a person is overladen with fears, much of their attention is directed inward and on themselves. This necessitates that they are generally involved in *internal considering.*[4] Internal considering means that one becomes self-involved with their internal emotional state of condition. This condition is driven primarily by the emotion of fear, which they do not control and direct, but which control them and play out of their own autonomy.

Some typical forms of internal considering may manifest as one thinking that someone ought to have spoken to you or said hello to you, or essentially almost demanding that someone should have treated you differently. Internal considering may mean that one is often offended as they assume they are being discriminated against for (usually imagined) reasons such as the color of their skin, or their dress, or the tone of their voice or language. A cumulative effect of this condition is for one to begin keeping accounts, which is feeling that you are always owed something by others or in general you are not treated properly.

Internal considering always leads to negative attitudes and a negative state of existence.

The predisposition towards internal considering may affect many, regardless of their station in life, their race, or socioeconomic status. In May of 2015, our First Lady, Michelle Obama, when delivering a commence speech at Tuskegee University, spoke about, "The nagging worries that you're going to get stopped or pulled over for absolutely no reason," along with the fear that, "Your job application will be overlooked because of the way your name sounds."[5] The unfortunate direction of this dialog was then it was turned into a race issue by the First Lady. It was now because of your skin color that you were not given proper consideration.

Internal considering, when becoming deeply ingrained in the collective of the populace and culture, manifests in demands of the populace that they are entitled to such things as, for example, free health care, a so-called fair wage, or a free education. Internal considering is grounded in the predisposition to selfishness of the individual, and to compensate for the imbalance within their psyche, they regularly engage in creating accounts of what is due to them.

It may be described in such a fashion including but not limited to the following characteristics which are maintained in one's internal foundation of distorted fear: I am owed something. I am the victim, you and the outside world are the cause of my problems. You aren't giving me enough. I am entitled to this, that, or the other. I am offended by what you say; therefore, you owe me an apology. Because so many are like me (likewise internally laden with fear and anger), I have to fight their battles as well and therefore engage in this martyrdom. Because you have more than I do, you surely acquired it by running roughshod on the backs of the less fortunate and the poor, and that is not fair, And look at me and how I suffer and everyone around me suffers!

And just so we're clear about this, do not confuse internal considering with what may be described as one practicing introspection—as introspection is akin to the process of one looking inward in the search for self-knowledge and self-understanding.

Internal considering is often identified in the behavior of one who is described as self-conscious. But the behavior of one who is described as self-conscious is grounded in fears of the individual in which they are fearful that others are watching them, fearful of how they appear to others, or fearful that others are always making judgments about them, and is a component to the predisposition of internal considering. If one is fearful that others are always making judgments about them, then it is a logical conclusion that one's entire foundation of who and what they think they are rests on someone else's opinion of them. As a defense mechanism an individual forms against self-consciousness, which is wholly grounded in the fearful state of the individual, that individual learns to incorporate intense anger into their interactions with others as a means to assuage their fear. It is repressed fear and anger that leads to selfishness in the individual.

A favorite word used by the liberals is fairness. They often will look for things and situations that they deem unfair. President Barack Hussein Obama often harps on the word *fairness,* but Obama's narrow view of fairness means the government taking from those who have earned what they have and distributing it to those who don't have (or, for whatever reason, made no attempts to earn much of anything) whatever the government deems necessary to distribute. It is extremely difficult to gauge and define what fairness actually means except when it comes to quantifying material things. That's when our government takes a strong-arm tactic through the IRS and other powerful bureaucratic agencies to redistribute your wealth.

To eradicate this unfairness, others are looked upon as those who must change ... change from who and what they are and alter their life circumstances as a show of proof to the liberal. Due to this orientation to the experience of life by the liberal; that is, this involvement in internally considering, the liberal may use any excuse whatsoever to justify their behavior because the blame for any woes they experience always lies outside of them. Something is generally going on that is unfair.

The liberal gets caught up in all that does not correspond with their demands and expectations. Whether that means interrupting a formal congressional meeting with shouts and rants, disrupting a formal funeral procession organized in the behalf of a fallen veteran of the armed services, blocking traffic to inhibit the daily activity of those who have no connection whatsoever with the liberal's issue, overturning and burning police vehicles, breaking into and looting private property, and the list goes on and on—so many of these actions may be characterized as unbridled selfishness perpetrated by those persons.

The liberal demands attention and the utmost of consideration from all, and if it is not forthcoming, their internal sense of well being (how they sense themselves) is placed at risk. If their demands to get attention are not met, their resultant behavior may cause them to lash out with fear and rage. And so, in order to further their agenda, they are endlessly engaged in this ongoing battle to force change onto the world around them; because the cause and the source of problems is generally always outside of themselves and blame rests entirely on people and the world outside—they never stop to be introspective and self-searching enough to realize that they themselves are the problem and they need to fix themselves!

And in the same manner that the liberal projects blame and the source of problems as coming from outside themselves they also project and expect the solutions to their problems to come from outside themselves, and in a general sense, can only be achieved by forces much more powerful than themselves, i.e., big government, authoritarian statism, and more laws and regulations to fix all these many wrongs! And, oh yes! The liberals must be in charge of all this because they alone know the cause of it. Once they fix it, only then will humanity be truly free—or so they persuade themselves to believe!

And so again the true meaning of freedom is expertly distorted and bastardized by the liberals and what they have convinced themselves of as a move towards freedom, is actually a movement away from freedom into various forms of slavery and subservience.

This quintessential liberal I just described, has little to no ability to attentively listen to a discussion or debate. They have no ability to 'hear' what you say. They are much too busy thinking of what they will say next because they are looking out for their own agenda. When asked a question, they cannot give a straight answer for the reason that their attention is focused inward upon themselves. Hence, they seldom learn about you (or the other person) and your point of view. You see, liberals, by and large, are very selfish and self-centered people. Much of their attention is directed inward—not in being introspective and self-examining, but directed inward in the respect that this is what is owed me—what I am due, as they are held captive by their own fears!

Pay close attention to news channels when a liberal and a conservative are engaged in a discussion. Liberals will consistently dodge direct questions; rather, they will try to equivocate, dodge, and redirect the dialog. It is because of fear.

The exercise of true compassion challenges the liberal's abilities because that activity requires of them to look outward—beyond themselves. Compassion requires one to place one's own selfish wants or needs aside and to keenly listen and observe what is going on in the world around them. When one is so oriented to life, this is termed *external considering,* and is a pillar in the foundation of true compassion. True compassion calls for one to step into the shoes of another and see things from their perspective. But if one is immersed in fear and guilt, then their attention is predominantly selfishly directed towards themselves.

Because the liberal believes that they are due full attention, and this according to standards which they establish, then they are eternally offended by word and deed which doesn't measure up to their standards, and hence will often assume an offensive position and be on the attack.

Who do you think is responsible for creating and categorizing specific words of speech and then censuring what they call *hate speech*? The liberals, of course! They have determined that due to their abilities of omniscience, they alone know that certain words hurt and offend people.

In the United States of America, our First Amendment and our right to speak our minds are under attack. In just a day or so immediately following the Muslin terrorist attack in San Bernardino, California, the liberal attorney general, Loretta Lynch, vowed to prosecute anyone who uses *anti-Muslim rhetoric* that *edges towards violence*. What does *edging towards violence* mean? Does she have any idea? Does it mean certain speech indicates an assumption towards criminality and the citizen will be arrested? Or does it mean that a person's speech will cause Muslims to react with violence? Actually, they want it both ways; in whatever manner it satisfies a convenience for them; that is, it serves as a convenient way for them to control your speech, and at the same time place blame upon you as your speech being the cause of another acting violently. For in fact, the liberals believe that often the cause of one's behavior (even if criminal) rests on outside causes, even if just words. If one acts up, acts out, or perpetrates a crime, it is the fault of someone else or a problem in the immediate environment.

The liberal believes that the mere utterance of a word is responsible for making someone feel a certain way which is generally discomfort, and woe to the person who utters the word, they are guilty. Often, a liberal will say, "I feel offended by that word." There is not in existence a natural emotion for feeling offended. So then, what's going on? The truth of the matter is that the liberal is angered by hearing this word—not offended. It is a curious phenomenon that the utterance of a word can generate so much anger in a person. And the liberal determines which words belong to the forbidden list, and the list of words on that list continues to grow and grow! And then, in a self-appointed fashion, they take up this manufactured issue in a crusade for others— whether others ask of them or not—because they alone are the arbiters of their own brand of relative morality. But if you ask the liberal directly, "Are you yourself offended by the word?" Some may say, "Yes I am" or may say, "no, I am not," but in either case only they believe they have the innate ability to know that many other people are offended. Even if they believe only one person is offended by a word, they launch a campaign to censure that word.

If (and this is the big *if*) one is free of distorted, repressed, and congealed fears and hatred, as well as free of superimposed fake guilt, words would not offend them. Not one word! Right here we must stop and once again engage in the exercise we did earlier. Do you remember? Go to the blackboard—do this in your mind's eye, and write this sentence ten times; *"If you are free of fears and guilt—words will not offend you!"* Following is a list of just a few words which may each be associated with a different race or color and deemed offensive (listed in alphabetical order so as not to create in the mind of the reader of this book that the author, this book, and the material are in any way prejudicial by placing any word in greater or lesser standing than another: *beaner, cracker, dago, gook, gypsy, half-breed, injun, kraut, nigger, paddy, Uncle Tom, wetback, et cetera.* And this is only a short list of words. Can you imagine so many words having the inherent power to offend!? Do any of these words offend you? And I didn't ask you if you find them offensive. I asked you if you personally are offended. Do you see the difference in what I just asked you? If you are addressed by one of these words, does the word make you feel a certain way? If so, why? Is there something you fear if referred to by one of these words? Liberals may respond, "Well, I'm not offended, but I know that many people are," or, "I find these words offensive."

Really, Mr. and Mrs. Liberal? How do you know for a fact who and how many are offended? Are you so omniscient as if by magic to know and perceive who is offended? Or, do you just assume a word is offensive to many and then use this as an excuse to propel your personal agenda, to vent your own anger or use it as a means to exert control over the behavior of others? Maybe you really are offended by a word, Mr. and Mrs. Liberal, but tell us, Why are you personally offended? Give us every single reason why you feel that way. If you can honestly say that you are not offended, then who or what gives you the right to take up this silly crusade for those you know little or nothing about? Is this just another excuse to perpetuate another one of your stupid causes with the real aim of exerting power to control and manipulate the masses? All of the rap artists, both black and white, who use the vilest of language in their songs, may find this paragraph perplexing. It would seem that the last thing they would want is for all people to be free of fears and guilt. If that should happen, then what's the point of their music? There's no one remaining to offend. No one would care for their music. Those artists will need to come up with and invent something else to earn a living with. They should then at least be thankful we still have a free market economy.

So, dear reader, and this goes for all, if a word offends you, it is your problem. Stop placing yourself in the position as the arbiter of word morality, as if you determine which words offend whoever. Do not make it the problem of the person who spoke the word nor try to solicit the support of the world at large to assist you to punish the individual who spoke the word and then proactively try to remove the word from the English language! Stop screwing around with the First Amendment! You know something, liberal, if you just minded your own business and went your own way, the world would be a much better place! Those who intentionally utter these offensive words with the willful intent to offend others, if you simply ignore them, they will realize that the attention they crave (because they didn't get sufficient fulfillment of love and attention during their auto-erotic stage of development, birth to four years of age) is not forthcoming, they will disappear of their own accord. But as long as you continue to give them attention, they will continue to play off of that and will continue to manipulate you by grandstanding and uttering words in an attempt to offend you. And then you continue your same silly crusade and foolishly fall directly into the trap.

A fine example of what I'm referring to is the recent media circus; the main attraction which focused around the name "Redskins," which, as many of you know is the mascot of the Washington professional football team. As sure as I'm sitting here, I assure you, it was one liberal who started this. And for all we know, that one liberal may even have been offended! I don't know who, but then, that one liberal spread the infection to another liberal, and then another, and so on—as it spreads like a contagion driven by repressed and distorted emotion within each liberal individual! Then, like a virus, once it hits the media, now countless people across America become offended, as they too are infected, as their psyche happens to be fertile ground for such an infection.

How is it that the name for the football team, the Redskins, was created six decades ago and only now, in the twenty-first century, this virus is just now breaking out and infecting so many? Was it incubating somewhere? If there is something inherently viral in this name, it would have manifested way back in the 1950s.

Governor Jerry Brown in California and many in the California legislature are infected by this virus, as he just signed a bill into law mandating that a number of high schools in California that use the Redskins mascot will need to drop that name and choose another. Many of the California electorate clearly sees the utter absurdity of this. But Brown should take no greater blame than the state Senate and Assembly which sponsored and passed the bill! Folks... do you get this!? And how do we know that all these many Americans are offended by that word? Because someone took a poll and by craftily wording a few questions to produce the outcome they wanted to achieve, they conclude that many Americans feel this way.

In actuality, it is the media itself which is the most vulnerable to this infection. Many chose to become offended and get on the same bandwagon. The perception is created by the media that a groundswell of support is at hand to erase the name "Redskins" from the public domain, but in reality, it is mainly the media who holds this view. Even Congress gets involved as if they have nothing better to do! But then, when Congress gets involved, one has to ask, "Is it real and genuine outrage by them—or, are they just glomming on to this issue under the false perception that a majority of Americans support it—and the Congressmen's efforts are aimed no further than to advance their own aims and ambitions, or perhaps to vent some of their own repressed emotion?" If the answer to both of these is yes—then that is reason enough that they should be voted out of office! FIRE THEM! THEY NEED TO GO! There are far greater issues than these which our leadership in Washington should be focused on. For example; the nineteen trillion dollar debt along with the even greater trillions of unfunded liabilities, the secret and unauthorized collection of personal data of millions of Americans without their consent—directly violating the Fourth Amendment; sealing our porous borders which allow illegal entry of unlawful immigrants, terrorists, drug dealers, and criminals; the assault on the First and Second Amendments, and many other issues that carry much more importance than dealing with the name of a football team's mascot!

Mind you, there are far greater numbers of Americans who would prefer this very stupid conflict would go away! This is just another example of how the basest of elements are elevated to a high level of importance in our society, often by those in leadership. These things feed on fears and guilt, it is about control, the bastardization of human suggestibility. It is about manipulation and fosters a climate of negativity. Fear often only begets more fear. When words become offensive, then many succumb to the fear of reprisal if they dare to utter the word.

A key element in the notion of internal considering is the notion that if all those things I consider wrong in the world of experience outside of myself could be fixed, then, finally I can feel good about myself. The propensity to internal considering may affect anyone in our society regardless of level of education, social status, race, religion, sexuality, or whatever.

Let's use our Commander-in-Chief, President Barack Hussein Obama, as an example. In the space of just one speech of his—and refer to any speech at random—count the times he says *I* or *me*. You will hear repetitively. I, I, I, me, me, me, ad infinitum. It is all about him. This is a man who is self-involved and self-centered. He is, in fact, a narcissist just as many others who are predisposed to internal considering. Narcissism and internal considering go hand in hand. Bill Clinton and Hillary Rodham Clinton are also enveloped in this same narcissist behavior. Count the times they say, I, I, I, or me, me, me. Surely, such behavior points to a lack of positive experiences during the progression through the auto-erotic stage of development. In a predisposition to narcissism of such great magnitude, can there be any true compassion in those type persons? It will be said more than once in this book, when the emotions are working in rhythm and harmony, then the emotion of love from the love quadrant may freely flow. True compassion entails that one has the ability and capacity towards objectivity to look outward with the aim to see all that is positive, noble, praiseworthy, forward-looking, and so forth, in the individual—all geared to the uplifting and positive outcomes of the individual within our society, and ultimately, the uplifting of all the population.

When evaluating persons such as this, one asks, "How does he become so laden with fear?" The root causes of liberalism are developmental, environmental, and psychological. An important developmental stage spanning roughly year one through four is a period when the child experiences the height of self-centeredness. But this is a natural progression the child passes through. If completed harmoniously, the child gains in becoming positively oriented to this physical existence. Though the child's experience is characterized by I, me, and mine, yet, this is a very unconscious state of existence— the inculcation of experiences at that unconscious state of internalization is that all life revolves around (me) the child. If this stage is completed rhythmically, the child gains a positive orientation to life. If not, if basic needs, wants, love, and positive attention are not satisfied during this time, the child learns to fear life and others, whether parents, caregivers, or whoever— all cannot be trusted. Therefore, these unconscious attitudes are carried forward throughout life, and the basic underpinning of these attitudes is fear.

Reiterating that the emotions are the drivers of behavior, the emotion of fear is the primary driver that compels one into narcissistic behavior. Does it occur to you to ask how the person occupying the White House and holding the highest position of leadership in the land be so fear-laden? Remember, this is the person who is fixated on I, I, I, me, me, me. As you stop to evaluate and reflect, do not complete your evaluation going no farther than the president, but go ahead and include all the many elected officials in the Senate, the House of Representatives, the Courts, the Internal Revenue Service, all the many government bureaucracies, and the many corporate and business cronies closely linked with governance. All of these men and women occupying the positions of power, most of them highly educated, generally appearing very confident, most wealthy if not extremely wealthy—anyone could assume that they really have it all together. Surely, they must all, without exception, be fine, upstanding citizens in many respects; and in context to the subject matter of this book, their psychological and emotional well-being must be at a peak level of performance and functioning?

But not so fast. Are all things really as they appear? No, they are not. We've already established that the drivers of behaviors are the emotions. Which emotion(s) drives these people in their behavior? Is it love of country? Do our leaders engage in the same zeal as our forefathers did in order to faithfully love and protect our country? Is our leadership genuinely angry at those who would attempt to undermine our Constitution, erase our common language, decimate our borders, or destroy our free market economy? No. I would argue that they are part of the problem. Because of their selfish interests, they are destroying these very things!

Yet, despite the destruction these self-serving leaders are wreaking on this country, many of those very same leaders who enter this arena of governance and leadership become very wealthy as a result of them obtaining and occupying some of the highest offices of the land. Take the Clintons for example—though claiming they were not wealthy people when they entered national politics in the 1990s, it is doubtful that, as Hillary likes to claim, during their early years in leadership, they had to struggle to make ends meet. Really? But now, their worth is reaching towards two hundred million dollars!

The Obamas had no material wealth to speak of until they got hooked into the network of Chicago-style government cronyism in the 1990s. A community organizer makes little money because they create nothing, manage nothing, and produce nothing. Community organizers generally not only produce nothing, but feed themselves off the public dole. But you watch what happens, once Barack Hussein Obama is out of office—he will already be a wealthy man and only become wealthier. Don't you care or want to know why and how this happens, as you yourself struggle with your job or business just to make ends meet? Doesn't it bother you that (the) Obama(s) takes joy rides in Air Force One, which costs millions of dollars?

Supporting the foundation and a driving force (emotion) supporting unrestrained greed is fear. Apparently, greed and the thirst for power (and let's take it as a given that ideology is part and parcel of power) becomes the object of their desire. But one of the primary emotions that drive these people to maintain their greed and power is fear. Many, without their material wealth and their positions of power would fear that their inner self would be annihilated. Without their wealth and positions of power, they fear they will be identified with one of those they often speak of (and I think refer to quite disdainfully) as an ordinary American. Count the times Obama and some others in leadership will in a speech refer to Americans as ordinary. Look up a definition of *ordinary*. It will read something like this: "of no special quality or interest; commonplace, unexceptional." Don't you, dear reader, become weary of being referred to as an ordinary American? Do you not see yourself as someone special in this exceptional country as well as in the sight of God in this very special creation? Do you think these elected one's see themselves as ordinary? Of course not. Obama looks down his nose with disdain at many Americans and sees them as guns and Bible clingers! Obama and the elitists see themselves as special and part of the elite class, and deep down look upon you with disdain. They need you only to the degree that they get your vote and are assured that you will maintain your subservient position. And all the while they feed you lie upon lie! And why do people lie? It is because of fear.

They will go to any lengths to greedily grow their wealth and preserve their power. And when the stakes are high and the risks are great, many are willing to lay it all on the line. The word of the day becomes, "Do whatever it takes." It is fear of loss that drives them to maintain their wealth, power, or ideology! Why do many liberals resist appearing on, for example, FOX News, and a number of conservative radio shows? It is because of fear. Make no mistake. Washington is loaded with fearful people! Does this instill confidence within you? Remember, you voted for these people. What were you thinking? Did you make a decision based upon clear thinking, reason, and logic when you cast your support to them? Or did you make a decision based upon your own distorted emotions? Were you under some sort of ether? Did you make a decision to support them based upon one single issue? Many in America are one-issue voters. One-issue voters are driven primarily by distorted emotion, not by reason and logic. It is often in this grouping as well that we find moderates.

And here I want to narrow down our focus to a tool(s) used by many throughout the ages to hold on to their greed and power—the tools they use are lying, cheating, fraud, stealing, and some even going to the extent of killing. Let's leave aside cheating, fraud, stealing, and killing for the moment and focus upon the behavior of lying.

Lying is likely the most ubiquitous of these tools used by the liberals (and liberal used here applies to the full spectrum to include Republicans [RINOs] and CINOs [Conservatives In Name Only] because lying breaks no laws (unless of course you are sworn under oath—but even then, the liberal may resort to equivocating as a means to dodge the truth, eg, "depends on what the meaning of the word *is* is," as made famous by Bill Clinton).

Lying has become so common that it is expected. Many of our population have become numbed and indifferent to the lying of politicians. The electorate for the greater part are well aware of the lying perpetrated by politicians (at least I hope they are), but many don't really care, they remark, "Well ... politicians always lie." The more power one possesses, the more likely they will get away with lying. Most politicians almost always lie. The collective common denominator of what constitutes ethical, forthright behavior has dipped to such a low level—as if mired at the level of a cesspool. It's as if so many have become acclimated to this low level that this becomes the norm and we no longer can recognize where we are. Metaphorically, if one lives in stench long enough, soon they forget the smell. It's like the worker spending the greater part of a hot humid day in the cesspool—by mid-afternoon, his awareness wanes to forgetting—forgetting even the smell of the awful stench he has been wading knee-deep in and working in the entire day! If one goes weeks without a bath, they soon become unaware of their own stench! It works the same with pathological liars. They become so mired in and acclimated to lying that truthfulness ceases to exist and lying becomes their comfortable norm. And all of you who repetitively listen to those lies, do you yourselves become anesthetized and indifferent to them?

President Barack Hussein Obama is a pathological liar, as are many other elected officials in the Senate, House, and elsewhere. Obama says, "If you like your health care plan, you may keep your plan." That was a bold-faced lie! There are many other lies too numerous to mention. Look them up; they're on the record.

Please keep this in mind, dear reader: It is predominantly fear that pushes one to lie. Yes, you may argue, but people lie to protect what they have whether in terms of possessions, power, ideology, wealth—but remember, it is fear of losing all of these things that compels one to lie! Do not forget that emotions drive behavior.

The question then becomes, how is it that so many people can succumb to lying? Where does the pathology start? As we've said already, distortions in the emotions begin in the early stages of childhood development. It is in the framework of early emotional development that the templates creating the *basic attitudes* are laid down. Very early in life, young children learn that they can lie to escape consequences or punishment for their commission of forbidden actions. They learn they may lie and manipulate to get something they want. Before long, lying becomes second nature to them, with not a twinge of conscience or remorse. And the more lies they generate, the greater becomes the need to cover up lies with more lies, creating a vicious cycle of lying. But why care, when everyone else does it? And the more they lie, the more accomplished and comfortable at it they become. And so the pattern continues well into their adult life, resulting in a severe pathology. And one of the greatest of misfortunes is that many of the electorate in our nation actually believes them. And in the next election cycle, they continue to believe the very same liars or their party associates and once again cast a vote for them!

CHAPTER 11

THE EMOTION OF JEALOUSY

This chapter brings us to the final natural emotion, the emotion of jealousy. This emotion may be easily misunderstood by many, and presents a special challenge for one to even recognize its existence in an individual, even though, once you fully recognize and understand its existence, it will become obvious to you. Be careful not to become confused in attempting to understand the emotion named by this word *jealousy*. Do not confuse your understanding of the emotion by associating it with the conventional use of the word *jealousy*, as so many today may understand it.

For example, many may associate jealousy with, for example, jealous lovers, or being jealous that someone possesses something that you don't. In these examples, jealousy is understood to be associated with envy. Envy is typically triggered and experienced within an individual when they feel threatened or deprived by the lack of a possession, a certain talent, physical looks and attributes, specific abilities, et cetera; and someone other than themselves possesses all these identified things or qualities that they covet and desire, in which case they might succumb to resentment and hatred of those who possess these things.

The basis of envy in this context generates (and is augmented by) the emotion of fear; and fear in turn leads to one experiencing insecurities and resentments, even to the extent of anger and hatred. Jealousy, the natural emotion, is not to be associated with, nor is it the opposite of, envy. When one suffers a dearth of self-worth, a lack of pride and self-esteem (or deems themselves lacking in material possessions, for that matter), deep resentments, hatred, and envy may fester and spread like a cancer in that individual toward all those who are in possession of those things, or even if they are assumed to be in possession of such.

A search of the origins of the word *jealousy* reveals the word *zeal* in various derivative sources. From late fourteenth century Old French, *zel* is defined as "passionate ardor in pursuit of an objective or course of action." Modern French evolved to *zele*. In late Latin we find *zelus,* referring to "zeal, emulation." A quasi-religious word from the Greek, *zelos,* reveals a meaning of "ardor, eager rivalry, emulation, noble passion, and also jealousy." If one zealously pursues a task, then that endeavor may be characterized as filled with ardor, passion, drive, and enthusiasm; and furthermore, "to seek, request, desire, and to pursue with devotion." A modern-day common dictionary definition of *zeal* will generally include descriptive words such as *fervor, enthusiasm, passion, diligence, eagerness, desire,* or *endeavor.*

Often emphasized in this work is the need and importance for proportionality in regard to the expression of the emotions in whatever given circumstance the person finds him or herself. This certainly applies as well to the expression of the emotion of jealousy. When behavior presents itself out of proportion to the circumstance, the imbalance shows forth as zealotry, characterized as undue or excessive zeal or fanaticism. In these instances, the natural proportional rhythmic behavior is tainted and augmented by undue distorted anger or fear, resulting in what may be described as fanatical behavior.

In a behavioral environment such as this, where an action is driven by jealousy and zeal and is augmented by distorted fear and anger, reason, logic, and common sense cannot thrive, and certainly results in distortions of behavior, and hence, what is termed zealotry.

Jealousy is the emotion that motivates, drives, and inspires us always onward to reach a goal or achieve a task. Anger is not the emotion that does this, although many will often speak of anger in this sense. Often, we may have heard it said that so-and-so was motivated by anger. Anger may be the emotion that assists us to get off our ass to engage in the endeavor and positively move against the opposition, or is identified as the emotion that will move us to take on challenges along the way. But jealousy is the emotion that propels us ever onward to reach our goal. It serves as a beacon of light to move us forward, to drive us to a distant goal. But this in no manner precludes that anger may not crop up along the way due to running into roadblocks and other shenanigans imposed by liberals and progressives as we strive to achieve goals.

Let's break this down to a very simple example. Suppose Mr. Jones has this marvelous plan to start a business. He's got everything well organized and thought out—the name of the business, the product to offer; he's done his market research and cost factoring, and the plans are ready to build his brick-and-mortar business. Each passing day he awakens before sunrise, hardly able to contain his excitement (the emotion of jealousy) in the pursuit of his envisioned goal. Then, it may happen on occasion that down at City Hall he encounters a mindless liberal bureaucrat who is an obstacle and a hindrance to move his project along. Now, he engages his anger (in proportion, of course) to challenge the obstacle (and not by being a yes man) to move against this obstacle. Once this particular challenge is overcome, his anger is spent and dissipated.

You may have heard it said of someone who perpetually appears very angry, or if they are perceived to be directing anger unnecessarily at someone or some issue, that they need to re-channel their anger, as if the energy that is the basis of anger can even be re-channeled. There is no such thing as re-channeling anger, as if the specific emotion of anger can somehow magically transform into something it is not. Anger is a separate emotion sufficient unto itself to do the job for which it was designed by God our Creator to do, that is, to get us to move against a challenge or obstacle.

In this particular instance of this individual always appearing angry, what we are witnessing is the perpetual expelling of much pent-up and repressed anger and congealed hatred. We've already discussed anger and the role it plays in the behavior of the individual. Each one of the primary emotions is designed to do a specific task, though often they may work in concert, each augmenting, embellishing, and modifying the others. Though Mr. Jones momentarily engaged his anger to overcome the obstacle at City Hall, his emotion of jealousy continues to be engaged in the backdrop and remains an ever-driving force to reach his goal.

The sports analogy serving as a laboratory to learn and observe the primary emotions is a great teaching tool, as we've already explored. A football player cannot expect to reach the goal of winning simply by perpetually engaging the emotion of anger alone. Once the anger is spent and expressed, then what? What is to move one to the desired goal of winning the game? The answer is obvious; it is jealousy and zeal.

Jealousy was the emotion which moved our Founding Fathers and all of those individuals in support of our emerging nation to move forward in the institution of, the creation and the realization of, all the founding documents, the Preamble to the Constitution, and the Bill of Rights, et cetera. Surely, if we could have walked in their footsteps, we would know that each and every day they excitedly awakened to the task that they envisioned and set for themselves.

Small children learn this emotion of jealousy at an early age—long before the intellect begins to form. At both a conscious and an unconscious level, as the child observes and witnesses various behaviors, they tend to want to model that behavior, having at that age only the primitive tools of observing and mimicking behaviors, that is, witnessing something and then attempting to imitate or model that behavior. Even with only those primitive tools, the young child may succeed in achieving the end result based upon a picturing in their mind of the outcome.

A young child may witness someone run very fast or jump very high. There is then an innate drive from within that child to duplicate what they see. And once the child experiences the outcome, a great deal of profound personal satisfaction may be internalized by that experience, which begins to create a solid foundation of—guess what?—self-love and self-respect in that child. Watch and observe young children in their movement, body language, and facial expression; you will see for yourself. Better yet, positive acknowledgements by parents, teachers, and caregivers compound the successes of that young child. Upon that template of learning, the child begins to build many other successes that will bolster his or her self-confidence to develop a winning attitude towards life—a winning attitude that will propel them to compete and achieve. All of these many influences during the formative years will continually serve as motivational templates that will continue to affect the person going forward throughout their life experience.

This innate drive to achieve—deeply ingrained in the emotion and structure of each individual—may manifest and be observable even in those young children who are severely physically handicapped. Recently, in observing a commercial spot on TV sponsored by an organization fostering aid and assistance to young children either born without, or having lost a limb, upon fitting the child with the artificial limb, the young child would then skip and attempt to jump, displaying all the jubilance and zeal one may imagine. Assuming that in those young children their emotional structure was untainted by repression and aberrant conditioning, it is the show of the resilience and drive that each individual is capable of, despite the intense challenges that fate may impose upon a person.

The expression of this emotion can be subject to great inhibition if the young child, or young adult for that matter, is laden with many fears, unresolved repressed anger, and guilt, as these emotional distortions will inhibit the natural unfolding of jealousy and zeal within the individual. Their drive and confidence, which should readily manifest from them from an early age, will be thwarted if not utterly destroyed! And the greatest of consequences is that as the child reaches adolescence, emotional distortions will prevent him or her from the lawful realization of their spiritual quadrant; the rudimentary strivings toward such which begin to manifest in the period of adolescence.

A young child in the earliest stages of behavior exhibits innate inborn curiosities pointing toward the natural predisposition of extroversion and exploration. Most of you have likely heard the terms applied to individuals that they may be either introverted or extroverted. We all have within us a portion of each. In my opinion, the ideal balance should fall in the ratio of 51 percent extroverted and 49 percent introverted. The child naturally and instinctively wants to crawl and explore. Then, once the child can walk, run, and jump, the child exploits these abilities to the fullest. The child proclaims, "Look how I can run and jump! See how fast I can run! Look teacher; see how fast and far I can throw the dodge-ball ball!"

These behaviors form rudimentary extroversion, creating the foundation of a winning attitude and formation of a competitive spirit in the psyche of a young child. But these instinctive natural attempts of extroversion and the creation of a winning attitude by the child may be hampered in a detrimental way by the adults in charge, especially if the parent, teacher, or caregiver is laden with fears: is predominantly a fearful introvert; is fearful in any manner of the child venturing out into the environment; fearful the child may hurt himself; sees the child as being boisterous or as a show off (and these things are generally projections of the adult or person in charge who themselves learned in their formative years that most forms of extroverted behavior was a form of showing off and they were reprimanded or punished), et cetera.

Most of these things are none other than psychological projections foisted upon the children by the adults in charge. If, in the view of all the various caregivers, a child shows too much energy, the unfortunate remedy administered by some school clinicians is to give them a prescription of Ritalin. That will calm and quiet them down! In the extreme, the adult in charge may inhibit or even punish the child for exhibiting such behaviors or engaging in such aggressive playground behavior. The end result is that the natural emotion of jealousy is stifled and the potential foundation to create the impetus of drive and motivation is destroyed. And of further consequence, the emotion of jealousy and zeal, just as happens with the other emotions, if subject to inhibitions and distortions, one will be thwarted from opening to their emotion of love.

It is an unfortunate phenomenon in our current culture that children in our public schools are being taught that winning is rather a selfish act. They are taught that one child should not be placed above another in terms of achievement and recognition. There should be no winners and there are no losers! Sameness has been added to the new definition of equality. Everyone in the graduating class should be the *valedictorian*. Or worse yet, strike the word valedictorian from the lexicon; it is unfair and it makes others feel bad if they are not awarded the same.

Judging from the direction the class curriculum and Common Core is taking us, the new threshold replacing valedictorian will be an average C student. The traditional recess period in school that many of us experienced growing up as children that allowed us to get out and run and play is in many cases being cut back if not eliminated completely. Traditional playground games such as Red Rover, kick ball, tag, and dodge ball are being eliminated, and in some extremes, even running is prohibited along with eliminating the presence of footballs, baseballs, and soccer balls! Can you imagine those signs of the circle with a slash through them erected around the school perimeter, BAT AND

BALL FREE ZONES? Yes, the school administrators and officials believe it's simply too dangerous for the kids. They may get hurt. This is a projection unto the child of the administrators' and teachers' own fears. What happens to the competitive spirit of the child? It is being thwarted and squashed.

At the recent CPAC convention of 2015, Donald Trump talked of how we as a nation have lost our winning attitude on the world stage and the need to get it back. He could not be more correct. Should we be at all surprised at these current circumstances of the loss of our winning attitude when the liberal indoctrination of children has been well under way beginning in the 1970s? If you want to know the basis of the destruction of a winning attitude in our children, you need look no further than the liberals in charge of our educational system. Jealousy and zeal is the emotion that motivates and drives us to the desired goal, and is in fact what contributes greatly to the manifestation of a winning attitude. If the foundation of a winning attitude is blocked, inhibited, and overridden by fear, congealed hatred, unresolved grief, and the artificial guilt superimposed upon us by political correctness, then there can be no expectation that the individual in our culture may function in rhythm and harmony, nor achieve worthy goals in life when mired in such perverse disharmony.

The predisposition on the part of leadership and those in authority in our nation is the perpetuation of this non-winning attitude. It is reflected from the top down of the leadership in our nation. It was President

Barack Hussein Obama who said to all Americans and the many business owners across our land that, "You didn't build that!" Apparently, you, the individual, your pride, passion, jealousy, and zeal, matter not at all to the president! The president was attempting to destroy the very pride and responsibility that comes with creating and achieving from one's own efforts. The message sent was that you, the individual, are nothing on your own! Furthermore, you can only survive and thrive by me, and the all-powerful state! As Obama proclaimed in his messianic, narcissistic tone, "We are the ones you've been waiting for!"

Nancy Pelosi, another representative of our leadership, is content that people, "Just quit their job." Her notion is that government pays for all, whether health care, or just to pay your way through life, allowing one to sit on their sofa and, even if only in their imagination, pursue their dreams. The liberal believes the rewards of life and recognition should be controlled and distributed by the state, exemplified in the distribution via our teachers in the educational system, everyone gets a passing grade, and via the immense net of the social safety net that was cast decades ago by the liberal Democrats to ensnare so many! The broad reach of this safety net only serves to inhibit and stifle individual drive, motivation, and initiative, and is a direct assault on individual freedom, and I will go so far as to say it is a direct violation of the end goals and natural heritage of all Americans, the foundation of which is grounded in God-given natural law which dictates that all benefits must be earned! After all, there are only so many pieces to the pie and we need to divvy it up fairly ... so says President Barack Hussein Obama!

The emotions of jealousy and zeal played a big role in our country's history from the very founding of our nation and through all the invention and innovation of the Industrial Revolution. Indeed, our free market economy and the tenets of capitalism were furthered by this innate emotion that manifested itself through individual initiative, drive, and achievement.

Was it not possible then that once our nation's founding had stood the test of trials on the road to nationhood, after all the experiences of anger, grief, fear, and jealousy and zeal, on the part of so many, that an intense love of country was fostered? What happened to that love of country? Does it still exist? Today we have far too many who hate this country and view our history, our culture, and our Constitution with disdain, even to the extent of altering history as it is taught in our schools. Many hate our country and what they perceive as our history of colonialism patterned after the British.

What would motivate people to do this? What would move our current president, Barack Hussein Obama, to return a bust of Winston Churchill? Could this act have been symbolic in revealing an attitude? Was it an attitude embodying an intense hatred of the British, Churchill, colonialism, and capitalism?

How is it that our Constitution, which all our government officials take a sworn oath to uphold, is now being decimated and destroyed? Then by extension, do we conclude that this hatred of all America in effect represents hatred toward a very basic emotional predisposition and behavior of our humanity?

But one of the greatest tragedies of our era is that we as a nation and a culture are speedily moving away from a rhythmic existence. We are witnessing a willful disruption of the natural expression of the natural emotions; the most innocuous expression of anger is viewed more as a crime; the emotion of jealousy (zeal) is clearly under attack, which can only contribute to creating a nation of losers. A climate of fear is being compounded by the bigness and formidableness of government and other governmental institutions and by the ubiquitous cancerous spread of political correctness. And the emotion of grief is provided no outlet for the citizenry, as it seems there is nowhere or no one to whom we may plead our case and plead our loss of so very much that for decades and centuries was part of our traditional foundation.

And the greatest tragedy of all, as has been mentioned more than once in this book, is that all the natural emotions must be working in harmony before the emotion of love may be fully engaged and realized. And with the inhibition of realizing fully the enjoining of the emotion of love, we may be inhibiting our connection with our spiritual self, and the fulfillment of our ultimate destiny, which is our return back to God from whence we came.

CHAPTER 12

THE EMOTIONS, DESTROYING MISCONCEPTIONS, AND LOOKING FORWARD

The emotional quadrant of the human being is a magnificent component built into this wondrous piece of machinery by the Divine Architect—God our Creator. All of the five primary emotions of the emotional quadrant when functioning in harmony and rhythm, serve to propel and motivate us to achieve and excel and will serve to allow us to accumulate countless positive experiences in this life and we will be blessed with a rhythmic existence. But when that rhythm is broken by emotional dysfunctions that will bring about emotional disharmony, we may only expect strife, pain, sorrow, disillusionment, useless suffering, and disappointment around every corner. The individual will be detrimentally affected, which will then effect the family unit, and from there the ripple effect will extend to the community, to the state, and lastly to the nation. And the greatest of misfortunes is the failure of each individual falling short of achieving their spiritual destiny.

Each and every individual on this Earth has all the potential built into this magnificent structure, into which are designed the components identified as the physical, intellectual, emotional, and spiritual, and with that the possibility that an individual may achieve their ultimate aim and destiny. How is it then that we get off course, and life, instead of being a challenge that each one of us may take on with enthusiasm and zeal, becomes an ordeal faced with an attitude of negative tolerance and fear?

For a number of years I worked closely within the funeral services industry helping countless individuals maneuver through the difficult period of grief experienced upon the loss of a loved one. Countless times I heard people utter these words in the presence of the deceased, "Well, he (or she) is now in a better place." First of all, these words were spoken in a very matter-of-fact way, as if that person had the foundational knowledge to make such a statement and pronounce such an epitaph upon the deceased. Furthermore, does such a pronouncement suggest that life as lived and as we find it falls short of being a desirous place of existence, even for one to insinuate that life may be dreadful, meaningless, or negative so that we must first die before we can come to realize a positive meaningful experience, and only then go to a better place?

And what do they define as a better place? Ladies and gentlemen, is there any good sense in this? To be born into this life, into this body, which is a divine temple that houses a spark of the Divine (a soul if you prefer) that each and every individual is blessed with at birth, is one of the greatest gifts we are granted. And along with that, to be bestowed the gift of life is among the greatest of opportunities we can ever receive! And it should be the driving force motivating each one of us to hold on to this great opportunity in order to reap the fullest of benefits—benefits that may be enjoyed to the fullest especially if having been worked for and earned—and benefits that will serve to enhance the life and experience of the individual and all parties involved.

Many often ask the question, "What is the meaning of our (my) existence?" As if at the end of the journey or perhaps sometime in between birth and death we will suddenly in a moment of realization grasp the ultimate meaning of existence, as if we can label it, package it, box it, bottle it, reduce it to a paragraph, et cetera. No. Wrong approach! Trying to grasp the ultimate meaning of life in this brief sojourn of ours is the equivalent of attempting to squish a bead of mercury on a pane of float glass with your index finger! Rather, the ultimate meaning of life is derived from the experience of life lived minute to minute, day to day, and year to year. That is the *sine qua non* of our existence. Life has everything to do with the quality of that experience! In various religions, an ultimate state of being or existence is spoken of, all of course, using different words; whether it's called nirvana, salvation, enlightenment, or whatever. If you haven't figured out at least a hint of it while you're living, that is, the meaning of these various states of being or existence, don't expect to have it magically happen after you die. Many sometimes ask, "What is my purpose in life?" If you fail to achieve the task(s) designed for you in this life, you will get to come back and try it again, except the next time around, the challenges you will face to achieve that purpose will be greater and more difficult. Why would you expect it to be otherwise or easier?

If a high jumper is attempting to qualify to compete for the national meet does not clear the bar at the desired qualifying level, would you expect the bar to be lowered just so he could qualify? Of course not! If the bar is lowered for one person, it must be lowered for all. Then, the entire notion of competing to succeed and win the ultimate prize becomes pointless and without merit. Rather, the bar would be raised to not only assure qualification, but to prepare one to win! For one to realize that to surmount the raised bar, one must practice and work even harder. A lowered bar achieves nothing, and there will be no reward. Well, correction. Only in the mind of a liberal would this be different. The liberal would continually lower the bar and lower it more and more until all could clear it. Then everyone would get a lapel button reading 'participant'. At the end of your life do you want a lapel button reading participant or a lapel button reading winner and high achiever? Which would you prefer? Would any one individual in this instance experience real joy, and the experience of achievement by surmounting the lowered bar? But clearing the bar at the increased height brings with it the greatest potential of reward as well as a sense of pride and jubilance. You must come to realize that those who would force the progression towards statism, authoritarianism, progressivism, et al, are continuously involved in lowering the bar on the masses. What do you think Common Core is? It is forcing uniformity on the masses—and added to that, a low level of uniformity! Why are valedictorians under attack? The aim is to reduce everyone to a lower standard; after all, we can't have anyone feel bad for underachieving in the educational milieu.

It seems there is a push in our culture to create underachievers. Why are efforts suddenly put in place to legalize drugs, specifically marijuana? Drugs are clearly counterproductive to anyone who sets their mind and motivations at achievement. In her essay, "Apollo and Dionysus," Ayn Rand describes drug addiction among hippies as follows: "Is there any doubt that drug addiction is an escape from an unbearable inner state, from a reality one cannot deal with, from an atrophying mind one can never fully destroy? If Apollonian reason were unnatural to man, and Dionysian "intuition" brought him closer to nature and truth, the apostles of irrationality would not have to resort to drugs. Happy, self-confident men do not seek to get "stoned."[1] Progressively, across our country, brains (and emotions) are becoming anesthetized by both illegal and (now becoming legal) drugs. Now we can call them all legalized drugs and that will somehow make it okay to ingest drugs. Why? How cynical of anyone to presume that our government wants to anesthetize the masses. Could it be that those drugged and anesthetized in this manner have nothing better to do than play computer games, text on their phone, and watch endless cable channel movie reruns and therefore are much more easily controlled and manipulated under a totalitarian state? Then, the authoritarians to assure subservience, throw them a bone now and then in the form of food stamps, SSI, free this, or free that… whatever. And if that doesn't work, use threats and coercion tactics.

It sometimes seems that this is all a careless game being played out. It is via our unprotected border that drugs freely enter into our country. Why is there not a greater push by our government to protect our porous borders and uphold out laws? This show of a complete lack of responsibility by the government has many implications. One justification of the government to protect our borders is to stem the tide of the flow of billions of dollars of illegal drugs from entering our country. Drugs are destroying our youth and culture. But the flow of drugs into our country is only one side of the massive problem; the other has to do with the huge market for those same illegal drugs. That huge market is composed of the many individuals across our nation who take drugs and are addicted to drugs for the simple reason that they cannot tolerate to live with their personal current state of being—or more accurately, their current emotional state. Those very people are filled with self-hate and self-loathing. They hate their current feeling-state. Their emotions, and specifically the emotions of jealousy and zeal that should stimulate excitement and drive to goal achievement, are in a state of paralysis. They are destroying their mind, their emotions, and blocking themselves from realizing their spiritual facet. When the emotions are out of harmony, the person is inhibited and blocked from truly opening themselves to the emotion of love and their spiritual self. It can't even be said that they love their drugs. Even here, this love of theirs is nothing more than the result of distorted, base desires. It has nothing to do with love! If their emotional quadrant were in rhythm and harmony, there would be no need for them to anesthetize themselves with drugs and seek to elevate themselves, that is, their feeling state through artificial means.

And on a side note, there are billions of dollars funneling into the drug trade, perhaps four to five billion a year. That money must be laundered to get into the banking system. Who is protecting the laundering of that money to hide the identity of the launderers and to hide the identity of those who are benefited by it? Do not be so naïve to believe that our government does not know nor that it cannot find out. It is the lives of your loved ones, your community, and the foundation that enables you to thrive in this country of ours that is being undermined … do you not care?

It is with the ingestion of drugs and alcohol that an individual will anesthetize themselves against their emotions. So very many people across our nation can barely get out of bed each day—some do not. They have no motivation, no zeal, no goals to achieve, and are filled with self-hate, fear, and rage. So they daily resort to drugs and alcohol.

Just as individuals have goals and desires they wish to fulfill, one may ask as well what the ultimate end goal is of the United States of America, as if to ask, "What is the meaning of the United States of America?"

This question makes no sense either. But it is relevant to mention that the degree of the strength of the nation is dependent upon the strength of the state—the strength of which is gathered from the strength of the community, which in turn is dependent upon those individuals composing the community. There is no end goal of this nation except that it maintains and thrives! But there is what we may call the *American experience*—and I said American experience, not American experiment! Surely, you have heard that abominable term, *American experiment*? This is how liberals see America ... as an experiment! Do you tire of hearing this absolute crap of the American experiment? An experiment of what? An experiment is what you did in your tenth-grade chemistry class. You and the nutty instructor mixed together this chemical with that chemical, all with the intent to produce an outcome. Maybe an outcome was designed based upon some formula or fantasy and maybe not. But once the outcome was achieved... maybe it was, or maybe it wasn't. Perhaps the whole thing went up in smoke, which then was the end of it. That is what you'd call an experiment.

Our forefathers did not engage in an experiment as they planned and labored to create the foundation of this great nation of ours. No, they knew full well what they were doing. Their design was to create an *experience* that would endure for the minute, the hour, the day, the year, and for all posterity.

Perhaps what all these people mean when they say American experiment is what is currently being played out by the liberals and our current administration and leadership; that is, erasing and leaving unprotected our borders, destroying our healthcare system with the goal to create a single-payer system, trying to sell to the people of the nation and the world their ridiculous notions and shoddy science of man-made global warming, decimating our Bill of Rights and the Constitution, and in effect attempting to nullify the principles and universal laws upon which this great country of ours is founded; destroying our free market economy and in its place—creating a nation of dependent people based upon big government socialism, thereby destroying individual initiative and freedom; downsizing and destroying our military when all the while our enemies at home within our borders and abroad are arming-up to destroy us, and destroying the most unifying and stabilizing social unit in this society or any society for that matter, the family unit.

These many outrageous acts of the liberals is what I would call an experiment, and metaphorically, it is no different than the nutty insane professor mixing and concocting every chemical element taken from the cabinet in the laboratory just to see what happens. It is a pipe-dream of the worst order! They have no clue what they are doing! It can only lead to a violent reaction if not explosion, and in the instance of our nation, the destruction of America as we know it! No, more accurately, the ideology of Marxism, communism, and socialism are based upon an experiment. This experiment has already been attempted in China, Russia, North Korea, Venezuela, and Cuba, and it is evident what an abysmal failure it has been. But the liberals claim it has not worked only because it has not been done properly, but eureka!—the liberals have discovered the formula. Now, even the whole of Europe is turning into a test case. Europe is being changed and transformed in the twinkle of an eye, in case you haven't noticed. Can you not see that Europe is in the process of being destroyed?

There are in existence immutable laws, universal principles and laws that serve to govern our existence. God created it that way. These very same principles are incorporated into the very foundation of our nation. Just as God created laws for the well-being and harmony of humanity serving to consistently and steadfastly guide humanity; so did our Founding Fathers incorporate these very same principles into the founding documents as a means to, "Form a more perfect union, establish justice, insure domestic tranquility, provide for the common defense, promote the general welfare, and secure the blessings of liberty to ourselves and our posterity." No, this has nothing to do with an experiment. How about this, liberal? We are all offended that you would refer to this American heritage as an experiment! Perhaps it is time that true conservatives apply some of the tactics against you as you use against conservatism. All true conservatives should be offended by your behavior.

Far too many individuals, now-a-days, rather than look to themselves for fulfillment—materially and otherwise—have come to depend on the government in Washington, DC; therefore, in a manner, rendering (themselves) the individual ineffective to action. What did I say earlier regarding what drives an individual to action? It is the emotions. Why should there be a motivation to action if the government supplies all? In effect, the government is denying and nullifying once again the emotional foundation of each individual. The individual is robbed of his ability to act, to get motivated, and achieve. This is in violation of universal law.

But the individual is not without blame. This relationship is sadly and sickly symbiotic. The government (and the leadership) needs the individual to help maintain their power and position, but in a turnaround slap in the face uses the people to serve as pawns that they can control, and will resort to the vilest of lies and distortions to maintain it. And the populace allow themselves to fall under this false security of the government—trading true freedom for ephemeral material comforts (food stamp programs camouflaged under slick ad campaigns using the acronym of WIC [do these programs not incentivize single women to produce children so they can reap the free benefits?], California-Fresh—liberal California is always way ahead of the curve … they actually created these sophisticated radio spots to entice people to sign up for the free stuff!], Section 8 housing, SSI, and all the other countless government [taxpayer] giveaways).

But along with that, they (so many people) have sold their soul by believing the lies, propaganda, and promises of security, as if the government is godlike. This act by the government—just so all of the many Christians are paying attention—is a direct violation of the first commandment, as you may know is, "Thou shall have no other gods before me." Is it any wonder that the liberals want to remove any semblance of the Ten Commandments from visibility in the public domain? How many have allowed the religion of liberalism to become your god?

It is well to review again what is happening culturally and nationally in regard to the emotions. It is becoming politically incorrect to express anger. If you do—you are a hostile person and will be ostracized, censored, or punished in some manner. The very emotion that the individual needs to counter the advances of authoritarianism and statism is being squashed through the tools of manipulation and political correctness. The emotion of jealousy and zeal is being nullified, starting the conditioning process early in the life of the young child—squashing the desire in the child to excel and to be a winner—and our leadership, especially our president, goes worldwide and across our nation condemning, criticizing, and lecturing Americans—attempting to make us all believe that we are a nation of losers, homophobes, racists, and xenophobes—even going so far as to viciously attack the very heritage, foundation, and principles upon which this great country of ours is founded. You all heard his words, "You didn't build that!" You are a helpless pawn in the eyes of President Barack Hussein Obama and can do nothing (may not do anything!) without big government! And by the bastardization and the compounding of the natural emotion of fear—this has become the most insidious of tools to control and manipulate the masses.

And one of the biggest lies of all intended to stimulate fear is the hoax of global warming that is being foisted upon us, as if we the people are the cause of it. Those who perpetuate this are liars—there is no science to support that we humans may be the cause of it!

The mean temperature of the earth might ... and I stress might ... be slightly rising, but there is a reason for that. Briefly, this is what supports their distorted notion of global warming, so once and for all you may know the truth of the matter.

A number of thousands of years ago there occurred a polar shift. Planet Earth tilted on its axis. Why do you think we have true north and magnetic north, and the same applies to the South Pole? What caused the tilt is uncertain. It could have been a strike from a large celestial object or simply the Earth's crust going through a periodic shift or adjustment, such as it has done more than once over eons of time from various causes—but not from continental drift; that notion is a crock of nonsense! Clouds are capable of drifting, but continents are not. I will address that in another upcoming book.

No, the slight global warming, if it really happened, is not manmade. How do you think it happened that the mastodon, wooly mammoth, saber-toothed tiger, giant ground sloth, and many of the other species of that era disappeared? And no, these species had nothing to do with the dinosaurs—they did not exist together, as that genus of reptiles ceased to exist millions and millions of years before the demise of these mammalian species. These mammals, a separate wave of creation long after the dinosaurs, were destroyed in an event of lesser magnitude than that of which destroyed the dinosaurs, but quite catastrophic none-the-less. How do you think it's possible that completely frozen wooly mammoths were discovered in the far reaches of the northern latitudes with freshly eaten grass in their mouth and stomach? This speaks to not only the suddenness of the catastrophe, but the suddenness of real climate change! Their climate was suddenly switched from a temperate zone to that of an arctic zone into which they were frozen in time and substance. Imagine that! Where the remains of those mammoths were discovered was once a temperate region where grasses flourished and the climate was mild. Hey liberal, don't you think the wooly mammoth had enough sense to stay where it's a bit warmer? You know ... sort of like liberal New York snowbirds migrating to Phoenix or Florida in the winter!

The position that was formerly occupied by the North Pole was smack-dab in a temperate zone, and the South Pole was somewhere in the south Indian Ocean. Can you imagine that? Now, after the polar shift, and due to the perturbations of the land masses—the dramatic plummeting of the temperatures and massive amounts of moisture getting generated into the atmosphere from the catastrophic events, these events that spanned decades of time—in North America you have all of these massive ice formations and glaciers that formed, filling the lowlands, valleys, and even depositing on hilly and mountainous terrain, but now, climate-wise, in temperate or semi-temperate zones. Then, guess what happens next? Because they are all located in what is now a temperate zone with a milder climate—as the worldwide temperatures begin to normalize—they begin to melt … very, very slowly! Now, you've got to use your imagination—(and use some imagination infused with some reason and logic), the massive ice formations begin to melt, though very, very slowly … slowly but surely. As a matter of fact, if it were possible for a human to stand as a witness to a massive glacier for his entire lifetime, it would appear as if no melting had occurred at all.

Let's create a metaphor. To do this effectively, we'll need to compress time. Suppose you have a big block of ice in your kitchen freezer. In the morning you take it out and set it on your countertop. You stand there all day watching it. By evening, you conclude not much of anything happens, perhaps a slight melting, a drop of water here and there. On a time scale of relativity, let that one day represent ten thousand years. But then, you leave it for a week and then come back. Let that week represent thousands of years. Then, there is a noticeable difference in the size of that block of ice. You just might see water pooling under it and worse yet, that water level rising on your kitchen countertop. Additionally, the mean temperature of that counter area may have risen a bit as the size of that block of ice diminishes. Do you get the picture, liberal? Time is of the essence. It takes those massive glaciers of ice a long time to melt. And by the way, liberal, we even had a name for that geologic aberration in our climate—it was called the Ice Age. It was global cooling to the max! And it was not manmade! Your manmade global warming or climate change crap had nothing to do with it!

Enough about global warming. Let's get this back on track.

What those elected servants of the people need to understand is that the government does not own this country; we the people own this country. All the while, fears are being multiplied and compounded, further paralyzing the individual to inaction, which serves to drive the individual to the security of big government. As already mentioned, but worth repeating, one of the greatest tools used throughout history to control the masses is the instillation and implantation of distorted fears in the individual. Remember how it's been repeated in this book how we were born with only two fears? We'll keep drumming this in until we do it ten times. Do you know the ten times rule? You do something or hear something ten times and it becomes ingrained and a habit? You liberals should know this very well; it's the same strategy you use in repeating over and over the mantra of global warming as you attempt to internalize that belief into the psyche of all.

If the natural functioning of the human emotions is thwarted and blocked, then one is inhibited from realizing and opening to their spiritual quadrant or being. Then, instead of knowing our true spiritual destiny, we have to settle for belief. Many years ago my esteemed teacher and mentor said to me, "Unless your emotions are in harmony and rhythm, you will be inhibited from realizing your true spiritual potential and destiny." Americans, you really need to wake up! You must realize that the state authoritarianism and social homogenization that we are speedily being forced toward is a direct assault upon the rhythmic and natural emotional functioning of each individual—and therefore, in effect, an assault upon and a denial of your spiritual foundation!

Remember what was said earlier that in order for love to flow and for you to be fully cognizant of your spiritual and love potential, the emotions must be in rhythm? As long as this disharmony exists, humanity will be cut off from their ability to experience unconditional love, and thereby cut off from their true spiritual destiny. All must come to realize that they have within themselves all the potential for self-fulfillment. Don't be a fool to believe that government is the answer to your fulfillment

What then is the meaning of believing in God our Creator? The problem is, we have far too much belief, and not enough knowing. Millions of Americans across our land sit in our churches, synagogues, and houses of worship, and what do they do? They worship and believe! It's very easy to believe. All you need to do is say, "Yes, I believe." One can believe in anything … believe in Santa Claus … the tooth fairy … global warming, whatever! And one does not even so much as need facts, reason, or logic to simply believe!

You may choose to believe in nothing more than change. Do you remember President Barack Hussein Obama's campaign slogan of '08—"Change You Can Believe In"? Do you recall the images from Obama's acceptance speech after winning the '08 election? Throngs of people with glazed over eyes, as if in a deep hypnotic trance, starring up at Obama. "We are the ones you've been waiting for," uttered Obama after winning the election of '08, looking down his nose at the masses—displaying an example of his Messianic narcissism! It didn't matter what the change was—just believe it! And nobody knew what that change meant, but it sounded good so they bought into it! That's astounding! I hope most if not all of you can begin to see what this belief in change has gotten for you and this nation! You were sold (and you bought it—you are not blameless) a bad bill of goods from this lying liberal president! Shame on you all! As the sayings go— fool me once, shame on you, fool me twice, shame on me. Obama did win two back-to-back major elections didn't he? Just to refresh your memory in case anyone forgot. And now we are on the verge of another national election. What are you going to do? Vote in another liberal Democrat so as to continue the legacy of lies and destruction of Obama and the liberal Democrats?

Believe that all you need to do is believe that Jesus died for your sins and you'll go to heaven! It's that easy! Now so as not to offend evangelicals, that was a facetious statement on my part. However, I do not buy into any sort of instant salvation that is built into a message composed of a scantily worded slogan, which somehow presents a formula that guarantees a fast track to salvation. This is dreaming!

"Change you can believe in." Is there much difference between that slogan and, "Bush lied—people died," in regard to any content of real logic and reason as slogans are designed by and large to only stimulate belief? That phrase alone has captivated countless people under its spell. Slogans are a poor substitute for reason, logic, common sense, and knowledge. The current administration introduced its own brand of dreaming ... The Dreamers! Do you remember that? Nancy Pelosi recommended all stop working and just follow your dreams! That's right, sit on your sofa and paint and dream! It's as easy as saying, "I feel." Remember those earlier discussions? Pretty easy—isn't it? And it's as difficult to argue and dispel believing as it is to dispel what one feels. And of course, many slip right into this artificial comfort zone of belief and try to convince themselves that all is well. But to know is very difficult. To embark on the path of knowing is a very narrow and arduous path. It takes work, courage, the ability to grasp and practice objectivity, and introspection! But the rewards are far greater than we can imagine. The greatness of the magnitude and quality of experience and the reward of the challenge one takes on—is directly proportional to the level of difficulty and magnitude of the challenge. Remember the earlier example of the high jumper? If something is free and given to you, do you value it? No, because it presented no challenge or work for you. Hence, you do not value it. Whereas, the greater the challenge, the greater is your peak of enjoyment and experience! All true benefits must be earned! All true benefits must be mutual! These two canons are universal laws of behavior.

In 1995, your president, Barack Hussein Obama made a statement. He said, "My individual salvation is not going to come about without a collective salvation. My individual salvation rests on our collective salvation." These are the words of a misguided, messianic community organizer. Doesn't that sound a lot like Adolf Hitler—or does it not at least form the basis of like dynamics when Hitler said in one of his speeches, "Deutschland ist Hitler—Hitler ist Deutschland"?

Either of these quotes by these two are the ramblings of a messianic madman! It is an attitude of either of them elevating himself to a greater level of importance than of the collective in entirety! The collective or otherwise called, the masses, do not achieve salvation—but individuals do! Remember what was said earlier about the judgment and evaluation which occurs to one following physical death? We pass through the pearly gates as individuals—not as a group! Is Obama referring to salvation in a religious sense—in the true sense of the word? Of course not. Do you think he has any clue what-so-ever about that? If not, then what is he talking about? It's all about him. He is blinded by his pathological messianic narcissism. As the biblical quote goes, "It is appointed once to man to die—then the judgment." And I believe President Barack Hussein Obama has at one time declared himself a Christian, and has also declared himself a Muslim, so in either case—he should know better. The collective does not go through the judgment together as a group. If it was a fact that the collective goes through the judgment en masse and all end up at once in the promised land, this would pose an even greater problem for the Muslins of the collective trying to sort out and divvy up seventy-two virgins—would it not?

You see, dear reader, belief is supported by the emotional quadrant; knowing is supported by the intellectual quadrant. And when far too many things that the individual depends upon come from the domain of belief and the emotional quadrant, trouble is at your door. This is not to say that the emotions do not have a major role in ones journey to assist our return back to God from where they came—indeed they do play a role.

Do you remember the earlier metaphor of the gardener planting his garden? All quadrants need to be working in harmony. Drawn from the emotional quadrant is the emotion of jealousy or zeal to assist us on our journey back to God, the Source from which we were born—and, by the way, from which you were born either as a male or a female in your earthly body, the sex of which you will remain throughout your journey on this earthly plane and throughout all eternity even to the completion of your sojourn back to God. No, there is no need for one to fret and stress-out about trying to discover their sexuality—that's already been done for you. All you need to do is strip down and examine your physical body in a mirror and you will positively identify what sex you are. It's so very easy!

Yes indeed, it is the emotion of *jealousy* and *zeal* that forms the underpinnings of the drive of what Judeo-Christians refer to as their faith or belief. Many Americans who follow a particular religious persuasion, often say, "This is my religious faith." What is faith and what is belief in a religious sense? It is that inner prompting that calls to us from within—that still small voice that calls to us to return to God from where we came. It is the ultimate destiny of each individual to return to the eternal home. It is the emotion of jealousy or zeal that supplies a driving impetus. But when the individual is laden with congealed hatred, anger, and layer upon layer of fear—then jealousy and zeal are thwarted and blocked and most important of all, there is no opening to the emotion of love that solidifies our connection with God. Surely, most if not all of you have heard it said that God is Love.

Unfortunately then, the repetitive and mechanical profession of faith or belief is just an empty shell with no substance and lulls us further into a sleep-state and a false security. Once, a business colleague of mine— during a discussion of religious faith, remarked, "I don't really know if God exists or not but none-the-less, I'll profess my belief and faith. It's my way of hedging my bets just in case." How many of us go through life willy-nilly trusting and expecting big government to take care of us and periodically (maybe once or twice a week) make a profession of faith or belief in the confines of our church, temple, synagogue, or whatever. Is that profession of faith nothing more than an exercise of hedging ones bets?

Toward the end of his life in 1959, C .G. Jung, in a BBC television interview on *Face to Face*, was asked whether or not, "After all your work and experience, do you believe in God?[2] Jung paused, smiled, and with a look hinting at incredulity, answered, "Difficult to answer. I know. I don't need to believe. I know."

Dear reader, did you know that 92 percent of those in Congress according to a 2015 analysis profess to be of the Christian faith? Only 73 percent of the general population professes to be Christian. How can it happen then that our Judeo-Christian tradition in America is under such sever attack? Don't you think some protection of our First Amendment should be forthcoming from our Congress; after all, ninety-two percent represents a super majority? What are they up to? The First Amendment should be protected by a super majority! Then, the only thing standing in the way is President Barack Hussein Obama's veto. And then, a two-thirds majority should override it! What are they all doing? Making a weekly appearance for appearances sake in their church in an effort to do nothing more than hedge their bets, or see it as an opportunity to form more business, social, or political contacts?

Regarding the Christian churches across America, surely by now many should recognize that our Judeo-Christian tradition is under severe attack by the liberals. Get this in perspective. The greatest teacher of all mankind, Jesus, was born into this earthly existence two thousand years ago to reveal to mankind the true purpose and the ultimate aim of human existence. If all are honest about the issue, we know very little about Jesus, limited only to what we know from the New Testament; and arguably open for debate—a few other obscure sources. Maybe this is why the socialist liberals find it so easy to attack Christianity; because they too know and understand nothing about it. No skin off their back if it's totally destroyed.

The only semblance remaining from the true reality and mission of Jesus' esoteric work is the Bible (though watered-down by periodic revisions), and from messages conveyed in the Christian churches across America and around the world—but many of which are under attack and their message is being distorted. And it appears that many people are willing to settle into a rather passive stance, and are perfectly willing to let the destruction proceed. Far too many are willing to say, "It's in God's hands. Let God do the bidding." The fact is, God rarely if ever interferes directly in the affairs of mankind. Did God step in and stop the murder of 6 million Jews? God did step in and prevent the roughly 60 million casualties and other horrors of World War I or II? Did God step in and prevent the millions of deaths perpetrated by Pol Pot in Cambodia? Why does God not step in to prevent the many acts of horror committed in the United States and around the globe—so many of these happening on a much smaller scale than for example the Holocaust? The answer is no—God does not interfere. If God did interfere actively and with regularity in the affairs of man, it would be a violation of one of the most universal and immutable laws under which we exist, that is, interference into the right of each individual to exercise the right of free choice. Even though God is the author and creator of all universal laws, even he cannot indiscriminately violate them. Yet, when it comes to the laws and foundation upon which our nation is founded, our current president who is an extreme self-centered narcissist, along with the support of liberal leadership have no problem to directly step in to violate, change, or negate our laws. This can only result in the destruction of the foundation of our country.

Mr. Obama violated this principle when he stuck his nose in prematurely in the events in Ferguson, Missouri, and Baltimore, Maryland. He altered the natural lawful flow of our due-process system, and hence, weakened our total system. If God could and would step in to interfere with all the various laws he created ... it could mean the literal destruction of the universe and our world as we know it. Do you understand what this means?

Metaphors are great teaching tools and to further explain the relationship of God to our world and the universe, I will employ a metaphor. In this case, let's say that the rules and laws that govern the National Football League are fully created and in place. The commissioner of the league will serve as the god of this creation. Then it happens that the commissioner on a particular Sunday afternoon is present at a game. On a whim, the commissioner suddenly decides that he wants to change some of the rules of the game for the reason that he decided that some things are just not fair. In doing so, if his decisions were extreme and brazen enough, he would in effect completely alter the game if not destroy it. The commissioner must take a role of hands off in the same manner that God does not and will not directly interfere in the affairs of man. But Christians and evangelicals do not be dismayed because there is a way that God influences the affairs of Man. All may take comfort in the words from Luke 4:10, *"For it is written, He will command his angels concerning you, to keep watch over you."*

The right of free choice of each and every individual is inexorable. It is up to each individual how they exercise those choices. I ask you, dear reader, how often in life have you been faced with making a choice, and instead of making the choice based upon your best combined intuitive, logic, and reason, you made the wrong choice or made the choice to take no action at all, afterwards, realizing that your decision was influenced by fear? Remember, in any instance where the situation calls for one to make a choice in which you may either choose to act, or choose to do nothing, both of these are choices. There is no such reality as avoidance as if you can somehow avoid accountability of choice! Choosing to do nothing is in itself a choice. An absent or no-vote by your elected official is in this category and they still must be held accountable.

Many offer the excuse and say, "The churches have failed us!" That's poppycock! No, go look in the mirror. You have failed yourself. Why don't you withdraw your projections and blame? Stop projecting the blame onto the most convenient target outside of yourself, and assume the responsibility for failure ... that's correct, you! The churches have failed no one. Really, the church is an inanimate institution, from which internally in those organizations—persons, committees, and boards of directors make decisions. But the churches, along with biblical teachings— which unfortunately have been distorted and changed; could at least serve as a last vestige of real hope and change, not the counterfeit brand hawked like a two-bit carnival barker in '08 by our current president, Barak Hussein Obama could nonetheless help usher in a grand reawakening! But unfortunately, in 1954, no thanks due to the liberal Congressman L. B. Johnson, when he sponsored a bill to grant tax-exempt 501(c)(3) organization status to churches, effectively preventing them from participating in political campaign activity which could then influence the governance of our country at a national level. I describe it metaphorically, the church selling its voice and soul for a measly twenty pieces of silver! Upon the passage of this legislation, a number of people called a point of order to the fact that this was a direct violation of the First Amendment, but their voices were drowned out by the liberals!

It doesn't take a rocket scientist to observe how the churches cave and submit on the social issues, one after another, and haven't you noticed that many of these very same issues are typically of liberal-socialist viewpoint? You must realize that the goal of the liberals is to change and transform our very culture, and an attack on the churches offers the liberals the opportunity to change our culture in one large swath! With the roughly 60 to 70 million registered voters in America being evangelicals, doesn't it seem that outcomes could be strongly influenced if these numbers could grab on to and fully engage their anger, jealousy, and zeal?

Once the process, currently underway, of removing God from the lexicon is complete; once the traditional biblical message is totally distorted out of recognition, and the identity of religion across America is totally changed—then, presto, we have a state religion made to order in accordance with the liberal agenda and once again, watered down and further diluted beyond recognition, except sitting at the head of control is the government. The government may even decide what to do with all the vacant real estate—formerly occupied by sizable congregations which have been destroyed by the change we can believe in. Even now, as we speak, our government has mandated homosexual marriage as a constitutional right. And the churches, one by one, will accede to it, progressively transforming the churches into the new mold of the state religion.

As it reads in John 5:39, *Examine the scriptures; in them you trust that you have eternal life; and even they testify concerning me.*[4] Instead of criticizing and attacking Christianity and sitting by idly allowing the process to proceed, why not set about to figure it out for yourself and discover the true esoteric message of Jesus' teaching, and make efforts to save this institution and the symbolism upon which our Judeo-Christian heritage is based? Be like the gardener mentioned earlier, get off your ass and take action! Once you get your reason and logic in order, engage your emotions! Make anger your friend to move you against the challenge instead of letting liberals (and yourself) make you your own worst enemy by allowing guilt to be heaped upon you accusing you and condemning you for the expression of natural emotions, especially that of anger!

During the recent generations, anti-Christianity clubs and organizations have sprung up in America, identifying themselves as atheists. The degree of the efforts to which these atheists will go to attack God and Christianity is astounding. They go out of their way to snuff out words, prayer, or religious symbolism from various institutions and the public domain, generally under the guise of the presumed constitutional notion of separation of church and state. The fact is, there is no separation clause in the Constitution. Freedom to worship is enumerated in the First Amendment: "Congress shall make no law respecting an establishment of religion, or prohibiting the free exercise thereof." Yet they (the atheists and liberals) have co-opted the liberals in government to assist them with their dirty-work. They continue to get away with what they do and their actions appear driven by intense venomous anger and hatred. All you need to do is stop and observe what they do. They seem to be driven by intense fanaticism and anger. Their entire life seems to revolve around this agenda. Where does the anger of the atheists originate from? Did Mommy and Daddy require little Johnnie or Susie go to Sunday school as children, and little Johnnie and Susie rebelled against Mommy and Daddy because they didn't want to go? Did their liberal kindergarten teachers take their side to support them? And now, they are grown up and they have an opportunity to vent and expel their long pent-up hatred and anger left over from that childhood experience. I'm asking! Seriously, where are the roots of their anger? And now these two examples of kids, Johnnie and Susie are grown into adulthood and in no way will they allow their children to be subjected to such indoctrination and abuse! Oh no, they will protect their kids from such abuse! They will pursue with a fanatical passion to snuff out any hint of religion where they deem it is unwelcome.

Here's how you deal with an atheist. The next time you're in the company of an atheist, ask them exactly what it is they're rebelling against. Have them explain themselves in great detail. Ask them to tell you specifically what they oppose. Probe them with question upon question. They should actually be flattered that you care so much about them to ask all these questions! But the fact is, they will probably get defensive. Remember, an atheist can only rebel against and attack that which they have learned and which exists in their own psyche, belief system, and mind. By probing, this can be drawn out of their individual framework of learning and experience. It's one thing for one to internally hold the notion that they reject religion and any notion of a deity, and then simply go about their life accepting the fact that others may have a different point of view, but to proactively and willfully go on the attack to destroy any notion of God and the symbolism as held dear by others—that is a severe pathology! The driving emotion of this behavior must surely be based in severely repressed hatred and fear.

Furthermore, regarding Christianity and the many Christians across America—stop your wishing and hoping that God will interrupt and fix things or that Jesus the historical personage is going to return to Earth to intervene. There is no second coming in the sense that Jesus, the historical man, will return, nor will the world come to an end in which case, many believe—they will then be ushered off the planet to heaven.

Ladies and gentlemen, think about it. If it were a fact that Jesus, the historic personage, the man, will truly return, how will you know if and when it happens? Will he be dressed in a robe with long hair and a beard as depicted in artist portrayals? Will he be Caucasian? Why not black? Will he be Mid-eastern, such as in the recent production of O'Reillys *Killing Jesus*? Just to surmount the ethnically correct challenge will be a real undertaking! You can bet on it, someone will be offended and complain about racism and demand affirmative action! Will he walk on water? A Las Vegas illusionist can probably achieve that! There are east Himalayan yogis who claim they can do that—and while they're at it, ask that yogi to climb a rope suspended in the air from visibly nothing. How will we know? Will he rehash and begin preaching what's in the New Testament, or instead, will he reboot—hit the reset button—and restore the New Testament back to its original format of hundreds of years ago and work off of that format? What was that procedure called that Hillary was going to do with the Russians? Press the reset button. Is there a reset button for the Bible? The Bible was not produced until what, two or three hundred years after Jesus walked the earth. Will he use a pulpit in a traditional church? Don't forget, you can spend the afternoon walking the streets of San Francisco and meet up with one or two Jesuses most any day of the week! What about that? Shall we ask for their identity? No, can't do that—remember, this is California—that would be profiling! Well, second thought—it's okay to profile in this case assuming that these guys self-identify as Christians! It's always open season on Christians!

The same sort of speculation has been going on regarding the arrival of the Antichrist. Presumably the Antichrist will be this charismatic leader who will arrive on the scene even before the rapture. As you may know, the rapture is the time that the Lord will suddenly return and call all Christians to heaven. The mechanics of this and how it is supposed to take place remains a mystery. Some speculate that the Antichrist will be of Mid-eastern extraction. Some proclaim that we've already had a number of Antichrists; Hitler, Stalin, Mussolini, Pol Pot, Idi Amin, and a few others. It has even been speculated that our current president, Barack Hussein Obama is the Antichrist. Please, ladies and gentlemen, stop your silly speculating about Obama being the Antichrist! All you're achieving is further inflating this narcissists already over-inflated ego! But *the* one and only Antichrist is yet to come, as so many choose to believe.

Dear reader, I ask you, just as it poses a real challenge for you to identify Christ when he returns—how will you identify the Antichrist when he returns? What sort of acts will he commit? How will you know for certain? Why not a woman? Why not Hillary? Then, suppose you all know unequivocally and positively identify that—here he is—we've found him—the Antichrist! Then what? Do you kill him? Then, does all evil suddenly go away? Or will it just create another power vacuum and someone else will step in to fill the void? Use your reason, thinking, and logic to evaluate this thoroughly.

Any vile, vicious, corrupt, arrogant, and pathological leader is only as successful as there are those who succumb to their message and leadership; whether succumbing because of fear, ignorance, heightened suggestibility, monetary gain, political power or prestige, or whatever reason. My advice to you is that if anyone steps to the fore claiming that (recall this quote from Obama in '08), "We (I) are the ones (one) you've been waiting for," or, "I am the new guru, the inspired spiritual being, the ascended master," or something along that order, I suggest you ignore them and turn and walk the other direction as quickly as possible. Hopefully then, that individual will be left standing alone twiddling their thumbs and with luck will disappear into oblivion. It becomes like a bad bill or motion introduced in the arena of parliamentary procedure ... if it gets no attention, it dies from lack of support.

The current seemingly downward-spiraling chain of events worldwide can only truly cease when all of humanity begins to awaken to their true spiritual destiny and the current disharmony and humanity's extreme un-rhythmic existence cease. And this transformation can only begin on the level of the individual.

What does it all mean, this second coming notion, which has been written of biblically? The best answer I can give is that humanity is at a crossroads. I would describe Humanity in a general way as totally out of its natural rhythm. Disharmony and negativity rule the day. And what is negativity. Reiterating from our earlier discussion, negativity is the state of being in which one lives their existence out a framework of repressed and congealed hatred, fear, and guilt. And to remind you, hate is NOT the opposite emotion of love. Hate is a repression and congealing of the natural emotion of anger.

To repel and replace this state of negativity back to a natural condition of rhythmic existence, one could characterize it as the Revolution against Negativity. Though these words were not specifically stated in the message that Jesus brought to earth two thousand years ago, still I would argue that this was part of his aim. Jesus' message was to show us the way back to God, from where we all came—all designed to direct us back to a rhythmic existence—the great message of which has been distorted, compromised, and bastardized beyond all recognition. People are responsible for those distortions ... don't blame it on the church.

Not so long ago at a local meeting, which happened to be a Tea Party meeting, someone stood and remarked, "We need to find someone who can step up to leadership." Why is it that very many continually look outside themselves for someone to take the reins of leadership? That seems to be the biggest problem. We have far too many leaders already in positions of leadership who are inept, power hungry (fearful), dishonest, liars, incompetent, and liberal-leaning. What I would say to every individual who expresses this desire for leadership, why don't you make a list of all those qualities and attributes that you admire and value in a person, and of which you would look for and demand in a leader. Then, once that list is complete, see what you can do about acquiring for yourself all the very same attributes and positive traits. Then, if you can aspire to attain all those very traits and attributes, it might just happen that your need for leadership will vanish, or at least, you may gain a totally different perspective of your perceived need for leadership or what you would demand from a leader! You just never know what new vistas may be opened to you. Good luck!

END NOTES

Introduction
    1. C. G. Jung, "Civilization in Transition," (The Bollingen Foundation Princeton University Press, 1957), 248.

1.   Liberals and Conservatives: Laying the Groundwork
    1. Taken from "Brainy Quotes" selection of Jeb Bush as found on brainyquotes.com. http://www.brainyquote.com/quotes/quotes/j/jebbush449979.html.
    2. Jim Hoft, "Jeb Bush Trashes Trump in Spanish TV Interview–
Promises Amnesty". The Gateway Pundit. August 19, 2015.
http://www.thegatewaypundit.com/2015/08/jeb-bush-bashes-trump-in-spanish-tv-interview-promises-amnesty/.

2.   Emotion vs. Intellect and Reason
    1. Katie Pavlich, MSNBC Analyst: "Americans Having Access to Guns While Terrorists are on the Loose Would Cause More Carnage or Something". The Townhall.com. January 9, 2015. http://townhall.com/tipsheet/

katiepavlich/2015/01/09/msnbc-contributor-
americans-having-access-to-guns-while-
terrorists-are-on-the-loose-would-cause-
carnage-or-something-n1940965.

2. William F. Buckley, Jr., "Interview with the Godfather", (Yale Free Press, March 2001), http://www.yale.edu/yfp/archives/01_3_ buckley.html.

3. Liberalism: "A Psychic Emotional Developmental Disorder"

1. Dave Boyer, The Washington Times, Monday, April 6, 2015, http://www.washingtontimes.com/ news/2015/apr/6/hillary-bill-clinton-fights- white-house-detailed-n/?page=all.

2. Rudyard Kipling, *Poems of Rudyard Kipling*, New York: Gramercy Books, Distributed by Random House Value Publisher, 1995.

3. *Diagnostic and Statistical Manual of Mental Disorders – 4th Edition*, (Washington, DC: American Psychiatric Association, 1994).

4. Liz Klimas, "Guns of Law-Abiding Husband Confiscated After Wife's Single Voluntary Mental Health Visit". The Blaze, March 12, 2013. http://www.theblaze.com/stories/2013/03/12/ calif-gun-owner-who-says-she-admitted- herself-to-mental-hospital-for-medication- adjustment-has-guns-confiscated/.

5. For consideration; any of you who think you may be suffering from a "mental illness" and have a need to visit your psychiatrist, psychologist, or marriage and family therapist, you will undoubtedly receive a DSM diagnosis, which will become a permanent fixture upon your record. Do not for a moment believe that your records are sealed and confidential— they are not. Especially with the advent of Obamacare, your records will be an open record to the brainless bureaucrats. The government insurer, whichever insurance company is left standing after (God forbid) the total destruction of many insurers and of our healthcare system itself, whoever that may be, demands a DSM diagnosis; otherwise, without a DSM diagnosis, the provider of services is not paid. Unless, of course, you demand that no DSM diagnosis be attached to your record and pay for services out of pocket. Also, demand copies of your case notes and records. You will want to read them to find out what's in them. But otherwise, now the 'government' has your record.

You see folks, a risk you take by going to your mental health advisor is that you will get a DSM diagnosis, and that opens the door for you to be deemed mentally ill. But there is not a definition of mental illness in existence. The government will deem mental illness as whatever suits the whim of a bunch of brainless bureaucrats or health-nurse-practitioners. Then, in any future background check made for the purpose of you wanting to purchase a firearm in your desire to exercise your Second Amendment right, for whatever reason, you may be denied that constitutional right because you are mentally ill. The liberals are onto this full bore (no pun intended). That's why there is so much expansion of mental health under the Affordable Care Act. Mental health will be another means whereby liberals can take away your Second Amendment rights, and not just mental health but through your medical health records as well. Senior citizens who are diagnosed or even suspected of having Alzheimer's may be subject to having their guns confiscated. And that applies to the healthy spouse living in the same household as the 'diagnosed Alzheimer's' person… now placed at risk to have his or her guns confiscated. You need to be aware and wake up to this. Even now, if it is determined that you are 'mentally ill', your guns could be confiscated (confiscated—even if it's your spouse in the same household who has been determined 'mentally ill').

There are already numerous test cases to demonstrate this fact! (See chapter 3, note

4.) Everyone needs to pay attention. All those very young kids in schools today who are being diagnosed with ADHD by these nurse practitioners, and then administered in many cases, those poisonous drugs, will never qualify to own a gun in their adult life because of their mental history; but then, despite that, if they decide to obtain a gun anyway, illegally, they will automatically at that very moment, become a criminal. This is very unfair—and liberals first and foremost believe in fairness. It is unfair because criminals—if they obtain a gun illegally—will have no change of status whatsoever for the worse—they will still maintain their very same status; that is, criminals. And this is just another example of how liberals help create an upside down world. Law abiding citizens are penalized if not criminalized for desiring to enjoy their constitutional rights—and in a manner—are forced into criminality, whereas criminals enjoy those same Constitutional rights even while they are breaking laws and get a pass! The rights they should be denied because of their act of criminality, they freely use and enjoy those rights anyway.

5. Foundations of the Primary Human Emotions

1. Tahira Yaqoob, "Sheryl Crow Accused of Hypocrisy After 'Limit Toilet Paper'

Plea". Daily Mail. com, April 27, 2007. http://www.dailymail.co.uk/tvshowbiz/article-450937/Sheryl-Crow-accused-hypocrisy-limit-toilet-paper-plea.html.

2. Jon Ward, "Juan Williams' son on why he became a Republican," Yahoo News, Dec. 22, 2014. http://www.news.yahoo.com/juan-williams--son-on-why-he-became-a-republican-040631869.html.

6. Individual Dynamics of the Primary Human Emotions

1. Elektra Records and Warner Music Group. Writers, Sandra Chapin and Harry Chapin, Performed by Harry Chapin. Released 1974.

2. GOP. Gop.com. Raffi Williams - Deputy Press Secretary for Youth and Conservative Media. 2015. https://www.gop.com/author/raffi-williams.

9. The Emotion of Anger

1. " 'Why Don't We Let Me Explain': Rand Paul Spars with Savannah Guthrie", April 8, 2015. http://www.nbcnews.com/politics/elections/why-dont-we-let-me-explain-rand-paul-spars-savannah-n337856.

2. George M. Lamsa, *The Holy Bible, From Ancient Eastern Manuscripts, Containing the Old and New Testaments Translated from the*

Peshitta, The Authorized Bible of the Church of the East, (Philadelphia, PA: A. J. Holman Company, 1957), 1170.

3. 'Young Oakland Girls Called 'Radical Brownies' Learn Social Justice Instead Of Selling Cookies'. February 10, 2015. http://sanfrancisco.cbslocal.com/2015/02/10/radical-brownies girl-scouts-social-justice-oakland-black-lives-matter-protests/.

4. Lamsa, *The Holy Bible,* 972.

5. Ibid., 955.

6. Christopher Hitchens, "One Angry Man", Slate. Slate.com, April 28, 2008. http://www.slate.com/articles/news_and_politics/fighting_words/2008/04/one_angry_man.html.

7. Associated Press. AP News Clip. https://www.youtube.com/watch?v= jrnRU3ocIH4. Oct. 11, 2008.

8. Lamsa, *The Holy Bible*, 957.

10. The Emotion of Fear

1. George M. Lamsa, *The Holy Bible, From Ancient Eastern Manuscripts, Containing the Old and New Testaments Translated from the Peshitta, The Authorized Bible of the Church of the East.* (Philadelphia, PA: A. J. Holman Company, 1957), 957.

2. Ibid., 1028.

3. Ibid., 671.

4. Maurice Nicoll, PhD. "Psychological Commentaries–On the Teaching of G.I. Gurdjieff and P.D. Ouspensky". London. Stuart and Watkins, 1970. Vol. II, 747.
5. Nia-Malika Henderson Senior Political Reporter, "A Different Obama Speaks Up on Race". CNN Politics, May 11, 2015. http://www.cnn.com/2015/05/11/politics/michelle-obama-race-2016/.

11. The Emotion of Jealousy

1. Michelle Hickford - Editor in Chief. "Is This the Real Reason Obama Returned the Churchill Bust" Allen West. Allen West.com. April 10, 2015
http://www.allenbwest.com/2015/04/is-this-the-real-reason-obama-returned-that-churchill-bust/.

12. Destroying Misconceptions and Looking Forward

1. Ayn Rand, "Apollo and Dionysus," *Return of the Primitive: The Anti Industrial Revolution*, (New York, NY: The Penguin Group, 1999). 99.
2. Mark Vernon. "Carl Jung Part 8: Religion and the Search for Meaning", The Guardian, 2011. http://www.theguardian.com/commentisfree/belief/2011/jul/18/how-to-believe-jung-religion.

3. George M. Lamsa, *The Holy Bible, From Ancient Eastern Manuscripts, Containing the Old and New Testaments Translated from the Peshitta, The Authorized Bible of the Church of the East.* (Philadelphia, PA: A. J. Holman Company, 1957), 1018.
4. Ibid., 1059.

CPSIA information can be obtained
at www.ICGtesting.com
Printed in the USA
FSHW011156131020
74673FS